Th

Last Days
of Israel

by Barry Chamish

Zionist Book Club   Jerusalem   Israel

First Edition

© Copyright Barry Chamish 2000

Library of Congress registration pending

All rights reserved. No part of this book may be used or reproduced in any manner whatsoever without the written permission of the publisher, except in the case of brief quotations in articles and reviews.

Printed in the State of Israel

ISBN: 965-7186-00-5

The Zionist Book Club
P.O. Box 10182
Jerusalem 91101 Israel
Tel: Toll Free ISRAEL 1-800-RABINY (722469)
U.S.A. 1-877-RABINYY (7224699)
Fax: 972-2-6259239
e-mail: perkins@netvision.net.il

CONTENTS

PROLOGUE

THE HUMAN PRICE OF RABIN'S TRUTH

My work is a burden. I know too much. I'm paying a price now and it can only get costlier. Three and a half years ago I wrote about Israel from two perspectives: the very positive—glorifying my country's achievements in various trade magazines read mostly by gentiles, and the very negative—exposing Israeli political corruption in my own publication *Inside Israel*, read mostly by Jews. The idea was to clean up our political system so I would only have to write about our achievements.

Then in November 1995 Yitzhak Rabin was murdered and I quickly gathered proof that our government told not a word of truth about the real circumstances of his demise. And for this I was vilified in the Israeli media, and twice, ugly protests disrupted my lectures. My family was forced to read front page newspaper accounts of my fictional life: I was a Holocaust denier, a member of organized crime, a follower of Rabbi Kahane (THE number one crime of the Israeli media), and worse.

But I could almost count myself lucky. My partner in *Inside Israel*, Joel Bainerman, flew to Washington in 1992 to research his book on the Bush era, *Crimes of a President*. Before anyone else, he reported on the Clinton/Bush cocaine ring run through the airport at Mena, Arkansas. He was the first to reveal the murder of Amiram Nir, a senior advisor to Shimon Peres and a major player in Iran Contra. He blew the lid off the involvement of Peres and Rabin in all that was Iran Contra: arms for hostages, drugs for money for guns for control.

While in Washington an "admirer" gave him a gift: a necktie. He even fit it around his neck. That very night, Joel's neck swelled so frighteningly that he called his wife to tell her something was wrong. Four months later he had cancer in the glands of his neck that spread throughout the lymphatic system.

Adir Zik is my compatriot in exposing the Rabin conspiracy. Because of his newspaper column and radio show, he reaches far more people than I do. He, more than anyone else, exposed the involvement of Israel's Secret Service, the Shabak, in the murder. Two months ago he called me to say throat cancer was discovered. He would have to undergo immediate surgery. I only hope that he makes the same kind of recovery Joel did.

There are dead victims of Rabin, and there are innocent people wallowing in prison. Arnold and Marilyn Cytryn are two American Israelis who resemble, as Joel noted, "my uncle and aunt." They came to Israel to live free lives as proud Jews and Israelis. Then in 1995 their son Shmuel was arrested and placed in solitary confinement by the Shabak for over four months. To this day he doesn't know the charges against him. We now understand why he went through the torture. In September, two months before the Rabin assassination, he publicly identified the provocateur Avishai Raviv as a Shabak plant. This could not be tolerated, because in November, Raviv played a central role in Rabin's murder, whether witting or not.

So two nice retired Jewish folks, had to undergo an agony few of us can begin to fathom: wondering if their son would survive prison isolation for no crime whatsoever. His "crime" was fingering a murderous snitch.

But he was luckier than one Yitzhak Newman, who made the fatal error of befriending Raviv. Within 2 weeks of Rabin's murder he was dead, a suicide they said. He was the only son of a widow, I'm informed, totally broken by her loss and just too worn down to pursue her suspicions of foul play.

As for me, here I am writing this in good health. I merely have to suffer harassment. I was interviewed by three American radio programs today. My line was cut off in the middle of all three. If anyone tells me it was all a coincidence, I'll walk away. I've had it hearing that statistical impossibility is explainable by coincidence.

For five years my family and I lived in relative tranquility in a place called Bet Shemesh. Then a pervert built a house behind us where there shouldn't have been a house. Every morning at the crack of dawn he would wake us all with the barking of his dogs. No appeal to him would stop the noise. Then he devoted his life to isolating us from our neighbors. Then we were victimized by vandalism, theft, threats and soon police complaints. We are certain he was planted to harass us and the tension did its job on my family in ways that could have broken us up at any time.

And I'm not even mentioning the opened and lost mail, the passport that couldn't be issued, the men with cellular phones standing in the street outside our home at 3 AM, friends who keep their distance because of perceived danger, the sudden difficulty in knowing who to trust...And worst of all, the feeling that the stakes could be raised at any time.

Because I have established a reputation, as *Ha'aretz* wrote on its front page recently, as "the leading researcher of the Rabin assassination conspiracy theory," people, at great risk to themselves put powerful documentation in my hands. In the past two weeks I have received the army records of Rabin's bodyguard Yoram Rubin, his driver on the night of the murder, Menachem Damti and of the State Pathologist who lied about Rabin's wounds, Dr. Yehuda Hiss. And I received a copy of Dr. Hiss's banned report, with all its lies and accidental, shocking truth intact within. When added to my hundreds of pages of police reports, hospital records, court protocols, private testimonies, I have built an airtight case that the convicted assassin did not do the deed.

The problem is I know who did. In February 1996, journalist Yehoshua Meiri told me who did it and why. I arranged to have his claims videotaped. So certain was he of his information, that he tracked Joel down in England to let him know the facts. Meiri insisted that Peres organized the murder with the connivance of the French government and secret services. He said the Americans and British were furious and unless Peres abandoned his French allies "all Hell would break out here." Which is just what happened as Israel was bled by suicide bombers within a week.

Yet, for a long while I followed the wrong trail, to America. The evidence I had gathered proved Rabin was rebelling against his American controllers during the last two months of his life and that Ehud Barak had made sinister alliances with the same gang at the Council on Foreign Relations that was becoming progressively less satisfied with Rabin's independence. It looked like a motive for murder, but I had to admit that new information pointed to France.

A French journalist, Pierre Lurcat, reminded readers in his Jewish student paper that President Mitterand had once faked his own assassination in a scandal that haunted him his whole career called the Observatoire Affair. The sympathy that arose from the phony murder attempt vaulted Mitterand's career to the top. Lurcat claimed Peres and Mitterand discussed how to do the same thing for Rabin to save his failing peace process with the PLO. Pierre told me:

"I was only using my logic, I had no solid evidence. Then the authorities came down so hard on me and the newspaper that I surmised I got it right. I was a law student at the time, I'm an attorney now, and the French media turned me into a lunatic."

Then I was reminded that Peres ally, the secretive French media mogul, Jean Frydman financed the rally where Rabin was murdered. And that Shabak chief Carmi Gillon spent the night of the assassination in Paris. And then there was that bizarre incident in early 1996 when Jacques Chirac went bananas in the Old City of Jerusalem. Peres had sent Yoram Rubin, everybody's prime suspect as Rabin's downfall, to guard Chirac. His French bodyguards informed him who he was and Chirac ran to the nearest reporters nearly crying that he did not need Israeli bodyguards. That he'd feel safer with Arab guards protecting him.

People ask me, "Why are you still alive?" more than "How are you?" Until now I've answered, "Because I know who did it and I'm not saying." Well, now I'm saying it. I'm on the trail to France. If I'm on a hit list, it won't make a difference anymore. It's murderama time in this world.

As a result of my Rabin work gaining credibility in certain informed circles, I am sent the lowdown on other political murders. For four years now the world has slept—

* while William Colby decided to abandon his hot dinner and take a final canoe ride

* while Vince Foster chose to crawl on his back so his suit would fill up with carpet fibers and then shoot himself in a park

* while Sonny Bono hit a tree and his body lay unnoticed on a busy ski trail for three hours

* while the only FBI agents to die in Waco were four former Clinton bodyguards

* while Ron Brown felt it would be a swell idea to shoot himself in the head then land in Bosnia for dramatic effect

* while a surviving stewardess and air traffic controller decided to follow him to the great beyond a few hours later

* while French police just couldn't locate that sneaky Fiat Uno which waited for Diana's car in the tunnel

* while a Clinton intern died in a Starbucks holdup where no money was taken

* while the President felt impelled to rush back from a holiday to Washington on the night his pretty adviser to the deaf met her demise

—and on and on and on. Clearly, it is a rather fatal idea to get to know the President from too close up.

When his bloodlust wasn't satisfied at home, he helped conjure up some excuses abroad. The hapless bombing of a pharmaceutical factory in Sudan just didn't do it for him, so a futile exercise against Iraq settled him down for a few days. But the thirst to kill just kept coming back to its master, so a phony humanitarian war in Kosovo helped calm the nerves. Next on his list is Israel, and my leaders will do all they can to help him out.

There is murder in the air in Israel:

* Former Interior Minister Arieh Deri suffered a loss a while back, when after his wife's adoptive mother refused to sign an affidavit testifying that she gave him all the money he was accused of stealing from the Israeli Treasury, she was run over by an employee of one of his cronies.

* Rabin's Deputy Defense Minister Motta Gur committed suicide because of his cancer. Only his doctor told reporters his cancer was cured.

* Two of Rabin's bodyguards also committed suicide. One of them Yoav Kuriel, did so by shooting himself in the chest seven times. A very persistent suicide.

And I found this out because friends of the person who prepared his body for burial contacted me. To prove the story was accurate, I was faxed Kuriel's death certificates. He died of nothing and no one identified his body. Now did I really need to know this? All I intended to do was investigate the murder of one human prime minister and before I knew it, I was tracking down serial killers. Jewish serial killers. In my country. One may be living next door to me.

During the Yom Kippur War, I looked at photos of Israeli prisoners of war in American news magazines and became a Zionist. I vowed to do my part for my people. I moved to Israel, joined the army, fought in a war and defended my country. And now I'm gathering indisputable, unarguable proof that the leaders of the country I risked my life for are tangled up in murder, either promulgating it, or covering it up.

So what's an honest Israeli journalist supposed to do? Most Jews would say, cover it up like everyone else. If you don't, you will endanger Israel's security. That may be true in the very short term, but over time we won't outlast the moral rot. The behavior of my leaders has nothing whatsoever to do with Judaism or Zionism as the Israeli people understand it. They have to be exposed and purged. Then the good Jews will set things right. That is precisely the view of hundreds of thousands of my fellow Israelis and their support—I receive dozens of letters of encouragement on a good day—is why I have carried on this far.

So now what do we do about the information coming out on the explosion of JFK Jr.'s plane? The day it happened I wrote that JFK Jr. was doing more than any other American media figure to get to the bottom of the Rabin assassination truth. I reminded readers that his magazine *George* ran a 13 page expose of the Shabak's involvement in the assassination. I suggested that this was a brave but risky stand.

Then came the tidal wave of data. The FBI Preliminary Report confirming the bomb on the plane and noting the type of explosive was used by certain foreign intelligence services. This was followed by Catherine Crier of Fox TV's *The Crier Report*, announcing that JFK Jr. was about to meet high ranking Mossad officers to get the full story on the Rabin assassination. Then *Ma'ariv* ran an interview with JFK's chauffeur, who happens to be Israeli. Then people started noting that Barak was in Washington at the time of Kennedy's finale in life.

So radio shows from America starting calling asking me to investigate a possible Mossad hit. They observe that the Israeli chauffeur was in a position to plant a bomb in JFK Jr.'s luggage... That Barak had an interest in preventing Kennedy from finding out the truth of Rabin's murder. And on and on and deeper and deeper.

Will I pursue this line? Is this beyond my intention of reforming my nation and finally reaching the ugly point of wrecking it...of feeding every anti-semite's wildest fantasies...of justifying every anti-Zionist diatribe ever written...of handing our Arab enemies the very weapon they've been seeking to crush us into the sand???????

I've always believed that truth is good by its nature and a lie is bad by its. I've suffered losses by pursuing one truth: what really happened to Yitzhak Rabin on November 4, 1995. I cannot make the same living from my conventional business writing because of Rabin. My family life is much tenser than it would have been without Rabin. A certain segment of Jewry despises me for what I am doing to their view of Rabin's saintliness.

But the gains are real as well. I have the admiration of the most dedicated Zionists. I enjoy status and respect from the Israelis I most respect. And they always turn out when I lecture. And they take, sometimes, scary risks to find vital documents for me. And there are more and more people like them every day. I can't let these people down.

And I think I will if I pursue the Kennedy line. If *The Crier Report* is right, and if the FBI Preliminary Report isn't fraudulent, then suspicion is going to be raised against Israel. My nation will be put in grave danger by our leaders and their intelligence services. And this time, I don't want to know anything about it.

CHAPTER 1
OUTSIDE IN

THE POSTMAN RANG TWICE

A few months after the assassination in New York of Rabbi Meir Kahane in 1990 by an Egyptian named Nosair, the rabbi's son Binyamin held a press conference and presented an amazing affidavit, which I was about the only writer to report. It seems the Mossad and FBI were forewarned of the assassination and did nothing to prevent it. An Arab had been planted in Nosair's political group and was now living in Israel for his protection. He signed the affidavit swearing he had warned his Mossad handlers of the upcoming strike on Rabbi Kahane and they coordinated a strategy with the FBI. The strategy was to let the murder take place.

(Had Nosair been arrested, the World Trade Center bombing by his cohorts may have been prevented, but I digress).

Nosair was not convicted of murdering Kahane. He received a short sentence for a weapons violation and that was that. Only pressure from some New York Orthodox Jewish groups forced a second trial, this time for the shooting of a postman outside the hotel where Meir Kahane spoke. For this crime, Nosair received a lengthy sentence.

I recall that the issue of the postman bothered me. We were told he was shot while trying to apprehend Nosair. Now why would a postman display such altruism when even Kahane's most fervent supporters were totally disinclined to get themselves shot by an armed murderer?

Fast forward to the recent shootings at the Los Angeles Jewish Community Center. Of course, the shooter had intelligence ties and spent time in federal psychiatric facilities. Now, he hates Jews and wants to kill as many as he can. So he leaves most of his ammunition in his car. Nonetheless, he shoots seventy rounds with no interference but hits only five and none fatally. The injuries are mostly to the legs. The shooter seemed to have been aiming at the floor. If it was fatalities he was after, he went about it in entirely the wrong way.

His gruesome task finished, he ran from the crime scene and shot to kill a postman. This time he aimed with some precision.

The post office is a fine cover for a specialist in bloody covert operations. If the wife and friends ask him what he does, he answers he works for the postal service and has his government checks to prove it. And brave postmen snuffing out escaping murderers is a convenient and almost believable finale to the perfect crime. Unless the shooters recognize the postmen and decide to thwart their plans.

If I was investigating the LA Community Center shootings, the first thing I'd do is dig deep into the past of the mailman. He could well have been another Officer Tippet.

THE SEROUSSI BRIBE

In the past three days I have been overwhelmed with correspondence asking for my take on Eduard Seroussi's "gifts" to Ezer Weizman. I was reluctant to dive into the subject without current documentation but will do my best with facts already available to me and by using obvious logic.

Of logic, we were originally told that between 1988 and 1991, Weizman received $450,000 from Seroussi as "gifts." Puleeeaaase!!! No one forks over $450,000 as a gift. We are talking about a bribe and to get to the bottom of the affair, we have to seek what Weizman gave in return.

Yesterday, journalist Yoav Yitzhak revealed that the "gifts" actually began in 1986, when Seroussi gave $6.5 million to Weizman's Yahad Party. Now we can be sure of two things: That kind of money is not a gift, it's a bribe and the bribe was political in nature.

Now let's do a little background research utilizing the talents of writers ostracized by the Israeli establishment.

Prof. Uri Milstein informed me that he has indisputable testimony that in 1977, President Carter forced the newly elected Prime Minister Menachem Begin to appoint Moshe Dayan as his Foreign Minister. Israelis were aghast at the choice because of the fiasco of his performance as Defense Minister prior to and during the Yom Kippur War. Carter and the folks from the Trilateral Commission and Bilderberg group who put him in power (Brezhinski and Vance were members of both organizations) had a different outlook: they were grateful for Dayan's Yom Kippur performance and wanted him in Begin's cabinet to take their position in upcoming peace negotiations.

When those negotiations began at Camp David in 1979, Ezer Weizman was Begin's chief negotiator. Dr. Yosef Doriel, the author of a brilliant book on the manipulation of Israel's economy and a longtime government insider, described the tactics at Camp David to me. Citing high-level personal sources, he assured me that:

> "powerful psychology was used on Begin and it included drugging his coffee. Weizman and Dayan were to take Sadat and Carter's side on all issues, isolating Begin and convincing him that his viewpoint on every issue was wrong."

Doriel insisted that Weizman's supposedly unexplainable switch from Likud hawk to Yahad super-dove was not his personal choice, but occurred with the overpowering encouragement of outsiders. One of those outsiders was most certainly the French multi-millionaire Eduard Seroussi, who transferred $6.5 million to Weizman's political party.

Rabbi Marvin Antelman, author of the widely admired book on the covert war against Judaism, *To Eliminate the Opiate*, phoned me last night with an observation.

> "A number of years ago I was interviewed by a Dutch newspaper and the reporter informed me that Seroussi had attended a recent meeting of the Bilderberg group. He asked if I had any more information on Seroussi's internationalist activities."

This is not the place to detail the Bilderbergers' sinister control of global politics. It would be best for the reader to enter his favorite search engine and find the information himself. Leave it be said that there are strong indications that Weizman is being manipulated by powerful outsiders. It is most unlikely that Seroussi pulled $7 million from his own pocket and handed it over to Weizman. He was merely the conduit for others who chose to invest in Weizman's political future. Most likely, Seroussi was the point man for the French corruption of Weizman, just as Jean Frydman played the same role with Shimon Peres.

To digress, Jean Frydman, the French media mogul, invested a similar figure, $6.5 million, in a campaign to promote the Oslo Accord in 1994. The same Frydman also paid for the rally where Yitzhak Rabin was murdered in a security services plot in 1995. Thus, it is very safe to say that the French had a serious investment in an Israeli capitulation to the PLO, and the payoff began in late 1989.

It was then that Ezer Weizman initiated the "peace" process with a series of illegal meetings with PLO executives in Geneva, Seroussi's base. In January 1990, these meetings were leaked and most likely by Shimon Peres...Most likely because Peres exploited the meetings to try and bring down the Shamir government, of which he was a reluctant coalition member, and force new elections. Shamir and Sharon fell into the trap and demanded that then-Science Minister Weizman be removed from the government, and an investigation into his treasonous activities be initiated. And they were treasonous by law because meetings with the PLO were illegal. Peres took Weizman's side and the government almost fell. However, Shamir caught onto the plot and accepted a compromise, which saw Weizman removed to the outer cabinet.

But the meetings with the PLO continued unabated. An Israeli telecommunications company, Solan, wired a direct link between Weizman and the terrorists and no one in the government chose to cut it off. Joining this link in 1992 were Shimon Peres, Yossi Beilin and Yitzhak Rabin and we know the unfortunate rest. As a reward for his incredibly illegal activities and silence, Weizman was named the country's President by the "peacemakers."

Weizman was well rewarded for betraying the law of his nation and last week, after declaring that he would resign the presidency if "peace" isn't made with Syria, someone leaked the bribes to journalist Yoav Yitzhak. While most of the media are guessing that Ophir Nimrodi leaked out of revenge, a brave few reporters are actually publicly declaring that their information is different. The leaks came from Peres because he wants to take over as President.

It makes the most sense. Peres and Weizman share the same French sugar daddies and were willingly corrupted in precisely the same way. Peres would have known about the bribes and as we all know, he has no second thoughts about ruining other peoples' careers if it means getting ahead. One example who knows but won't tell is Yitzhak Rabin.

5

JEWS FOR HAIDER

Once again the mostly gentile powers that be of the New World Order have set up Jews for a fall in Europe. The last time, they placed Jews like Rubin, Cohen, Berger and Albright (whether she recalls it or not) in the visible front line of the atrocities committed against Serbs during the Kosovo War. This time they have us leading the unpopular international protest against the legitimately elected Austrian Freedom Party leader Joerge Haider.

Haider's real "crimes" are that he is anti-EU, anti-NATO, anti-Euro and anti-immigration, a fine package that makes him anti-New World Order. So the Jewish sympathy card has been pulled out to bring him down. Some naive Jews have been sucked in by the organized media barrage against Haider and are playing along. The vast majority are entirely apathetic to Austrian politics, Haider notwithstanding. But the latter will face the same resentment for interfering with a sovereign nation's political choice as the former. The process is called creating anti-semitism. The methods are well known, and all are being applied to this issue.

Let me state early on that the Austrians are my least favorite people in the world. They were the most vehement of all Nazis and I will never forget the images of Jews being forced to clean the streets of Vienna with their tongues. My good friend, the Orthodox rabbi Mitchell Herczeg, tells me that the only country in the world today where he has felt an overall hatred towards him is Austria, and others who enter the place in Orthodox garb say the same thing. There isn't nearly enough regret in Austria for its crimes against my people.

That said, the campaign against Haider has nothing to do with me as a Jew. The fact that a proud Jew is a Freedom Party parliamentary member makes a mockery of Haider's alleged anti-semitism in the first place. I am satisfied with his apology for past remarks that could have been construed as pro-nazi—he didn't have to apologize, he did, it's enough for me—as I am with his public request to visit Israel to set matters straight. He's welcome in my country as far as I'm concerned.

He does not represent Europe's real threat to Israel, which comes from the very people attacking him. It has been Europe's socialists and Left which have been Israel's most dedicated enemies for over a generation. It was the Jewish leader of the Socialist International, the longtime Austrian President Bruno Kreisky, who led the campaign against Israel worldwide during the 1970s and 80s. It was he who constantly demeaned the honorable Israeli Prime Minister Menachem Begin, calling him such memorable epithets as "a village shopkeeper."

The real anti-semites in Europe are Robin Cooke, who let his true feelings out during recent visits to Israel and Gaza; the French Foreign Ministry, led by the notorious Roland Dumas, which has been secretly colluding with Syria for the past decade to remove Israel from the Golan Heights, Israeli security be damned; it is the Italian Communist Party, which has excused and applauded Arab terrorism against Jews for the past thirty years; and so on. Those who despise Haider despise Israel and that is no coincidence. That they are using Israel and the Jews to spearhead their plan to undermine, then overthrow him, is no less a coincidence.

So far, I have not come across one pro-PLO or pro-Syrian comment by Haider. But the few concerned Austrians roused to protest him are of the style and type who would justify any Arab bloodshed against my country. If, God forbid, I had to make such a choice, I would trust my country's future more in Haider's hands than those of his most vocal opponents.

So why must my people be so cynically used, and why must the weakling leader of Israel, Ehud Barak, be placed at the forefront of the anti-Haider movement by his superiors in Europe and America? It all comes down to immigration.

My friend Joel Bainerman has made two trips to Holland in the past year, and he is visiting there right now. He told me that the same incident occurred over and over again to him. He would be walking with his Dutch business associates, they would pass groups of East Asian or African immigrants and they would say, "In twenty years there won't be a Dutch people anymore. Two thousand years of nation-building will be gone in a generation."

If one's goal is to destroy nations in order to build a one continent, then a one world government, attacking the very genetic foundations of the nations' peoples is the best way to go about things. What will follow will be the inevitable loss of harmony, patriotism, language and culture. To assure that the plan goes through unobstructed, those who express fear of the situation, of the loss of their national integrity, are branded racist. An organized media will wreck the reputation of any person honest enough to express his misgivings about over-immigration, and Haider will remain a lesson for any future public figure, no matter how unbigoted and sincere; if he dares question immigration policy, he will be equated with Hitler in every nation on the planet.

Haider is no ignorant skinhead; 27% of a well-educated nation voted for him and the more Israel and the Jews fight him, the more his popularity will rise...and the more Europeans will resent my people for butting in where they don't belong.

BEWARE LIEBERMAN

VP Candidate Joseph Lieberman is a member of the Council on Foreign Relations (CFR), as are Dick Cheney, and Al Gore. The only candidate not on the members' list is G.W. Bush Jr. who is a member by proxy. His grandfather Prescott was a CFR pioneer, while dad, George Sr. was an executive of the accursed cult whose aim is a one world government. With only 3000 members, it is clear that only CFR members and loyalists may become President. Last time around the figures were the same, Gore, Dole and Clinton were CFR members. The story has been similar for the past two generations.

Rabbi Marvin Antelman has been fighting the CFR for three decades. In 1972, he submitted a proposal to the Rabbinical Council of America to condemn the CFR and prevent its members from infiltrating Jewish institutions. In 1974, his book *To Eliminate the Opiate* was published. Long considered a classic in many circles, the book exposed the CFR's program to wipe out Judaism by planting its members throughout Jewish media, charitable and educational institutes.

He called last night to tell me that, "I just went through the CFR roster. Lieberman's name is on the membership list. We're being sold a bill of goods again."

The CFR's Middle East Task Force Report of July 1997 spells out the organization's position in no uncertain terms; Israel must return to its undefendable 1948 borders and Jerusalem is to be divided into two national capitals. Rabbi Antelman thus doubts the authenticity of Lieberman's commitment to Orthodox Jewry.

> "How can you be Orthodox and belong to an organization which promotes the division of Jerusalem and which, in the past, has financially backed such irreligious movements as communism and nazism?" he asks. "The CFR's purpose is to promote and arm violent and disruptive national movements in order to upset the world's status quo and replace it with their alternative world order. There is no place within for a religious Jew unless he is dangerous window dressing."

What that will mean for Israel is more suicidal concessions with American Jews unable to accuse the administration of being anti-Israel. The same trick was used in 1972 when CFR executive Henry Kissinger was named Secretary of State. Equally proud of

Kissinger as they are of Lieberman today, the Jewish community could not accuse the administration of deliberately trying to eliminate Israel in the Yom Kippur War of 1973, nor could they find sinister motives for the isolation of Israel in the peace process which followed it.

This time around, not only does the current "peace" process get a boost, so does the Hillary Clinton campaign for a New York senatorial seat. And the Jews, so excited by Lieberman's nomination, as usual, do not suspect how cynically they are being set up.

The signs are there for anyone to see. Last year Lieberman welcomed Arafat to America and even prayed for the success of his mission. And he initiated a publicized letter to President Clinton nixing any chance of CFR victim Jonathan Pollard's release from prison. As *The Jerusalem Post* noted, Pollard's website has long accused Lieberman of being "a willing tool of the CIA."

Sooner or later Lieberman's possible dual allegiance to America and Israel will become a debating point. Observes Antelman, "And that will miss the real issue, which is Lieberman's allegiance to the CFR. It will prove stronger than all his sentimental ties to America, Israel and to Judaism itself."

THE RABIN MURDER EXPRESS ROLLS ALONG—
THIS TIME IT'S ELIAHU BEN-ELISSAR

A week after PM Ehud Barak fired seven foreign diplomats, one of them, the Israeli ambassador to France, Eliahu Ben-Elissar was dead. According to *The Jerusalem Post*:

> "The circumstances of his death have sparked a number of rumors. 'The rumors surrounding his death are vicious,' a Foreign Ministry spokesman said."

And why shouldn't they be? Here is what we have been told. In the morning of Saturday, August 12, Ben-Elissar arrived at the Hotel Atala, a rather obscure and unimposing establishment that for years has been where the Israeli embassy has put up guests and arranged meetings. He was not accompanied by his bodyguards. As *Ma'ariv* observed:

> "In Israel, questions are being asked about the ambassador's security arrangements. The central question is why Ben-Elissar arrived without his bodyguards, which according to regulations, must accompany him every time he leaves his apartment."

Missing also, was his French police protection. According to *The Jerusalem Post*, "A special branch of the French Police usually shadows every move made by VIPs at risk." But Ben-Elissar's Israeli and French bodyguards were not anywhere near him, "apparently at his own request." At noon, Ben-Elissar, aged 68, told hotel staff he wasn't feeling well. By 1:30 he was dead of a heart attack, though according to one embassy employee quoted by *Ma'ariv*, "He was in the peak of health. He never complained of poor health and was rarely ill."

French police conducted a most perfunctory investigation and within hours declared Ben-Elissar's death natural. Of course, these same police similarly concluded that Princess Diana died in "an accident." Call it a co-incidence, but on the day of Ben-Elissar's death, I received the following e-mail, paraphrased because of the halting English:

> "I just read your article, 'Rigged' How did you know about the French connection to Rabin's murder? I discovered it three months

ago after a discussion with an agent of French Intelligence. It's all true."

I suspect so did Ben-Elissar. The only possible reason he would have interrupted his sabbath to go to the hotel was to meet someone. Yet not one press report reached this obvious conclusion, thus no one is asking who the ambassador met on his final morning. Whoever he was, either he was a guest of the Israeli embassy staying at the hotel or was familiar enough with embassy habits to choose it for a fatal meeting.

The following scenario makes the most sense to me with the paucity of information available. At least one French intelligence official has been leaking the fact that his government helped murder Yitzhak Rabin in order to place their agent Shimon Peres in the Israeli Prime Minister's office. Word reached Barak that Ben-Elissar had been apprised of the truth and he had him recalled. To avert suspicion, he recalled six other diplomats at the same time. But in his last days in Paris, Ben-Elissar continued gathering the facts.

Ben-Elissar was lured to the hotel with the promise of additional proofs and told that he must arrive without any security. Once there, the "informant" spiked his coffee or utilized another means to initiate a mortal cardiac arrest.

One more influential individual who knew too much about Rabin's assassination then bit the dust. And when will it all end?

* * *

The panic to stanch the Rabin truth can be gauged by my experience. Last month, an attempt on my life was made by sabotaging my car. The next day, I had a long talk with my insurance adjuster who explained in detail how the sabotage was accomplished. Two days ago, the insurance company sent a letter explaining my accident was the result of mechanical failure. I phoned my insurance company and demanded the adjuster's report. It has not been forthcoming. Photographs of the car's damage, sent last week from Bet Shemesh, have not arrived. Nor have photographs of police surrounding me at a Tel Aviv rally, sent two weeks ago by a correspondent, arrived.

Yesterday morning there was a knock on my door. I looked through the keyhole and saw a husky young man. I asked who he was.

12

He answered, "A friend." I replied, "Which friend?" Then he ran away. I opened the door after a few seconds and he was nowhere to be seen.

The Rabin truth must emerge before more people, yours truly included, are murdered.

'99 ELECTION SHENANIGANS

ELECTION HUSH WORDS

The Israeli election campaign is winding down and it's safe to call it the most boring in anyone's memory. There are two reasons for this: the public is sick of its politicians, and the media has used all its power to hush the real issues. Three examples of two word phrases not discussed openly give a hint of how public opinion is being molded.

1. Arab Vote: If Barak wins—and polls have him leading by 8-9%— it will be because 95% of the Arab votes will go to him. With 18% of the population, the Arabs can now keep the Left in power virtually forever. To sum the issue up, the majority of Jews—it looks like about 56%—will vote Netanyahu, while a Jewish minority will support Barak. In an election to determine the leader of the Zionist Knesset, Barak will likely be elected and then be totally dependent for his continuing power on anti-Zionist voters.

Now try and find this central issue discussed in Israeli newspapers or over Israeli airwaves. The media justify their hush-up by calling the issue racist. However, its real motivation is ignoring any debate, which could give Netanyahu an edge.

2. Dirty Courts: The talk on the street is how the Israeli judicial system suddenly took a stand against political corruption since the election campaign began. First, the guardian of Israeli ethics, State Comptroller Miriam Ben Porat, was not allowed to complete her investigation of Ehud Barak's role in the Tze'elim Bet disaster. If he was not personally responsible for the deaths of five soldiers in a training accident in 1992 at the Tze'elim army base as the highest ranking officer on the site, his neglect of the wounded and his contradictory testimonies at two commissions of inquiry more than suggested that he was in deep political hot water...However, a new State Comptroller, commonly known as Goldberg, conducted a last minute investigation of his own and found that Barak was right as rain.

15

Then came the flood of indictments against the Likud. Justice Minister Tzahi Hanegbi and Foreign Minister Ariel Sharon were on the way to indictments for bribery—in Sharon's case for a crime supposedly committed in 1982—while former chief Netanyahu aide Avigdor Lieberman allegedly threatened the honest working of the police force with his racist and inflammatory remarks about it. Three kingpins in a row were toppled by the attorney general and the Israeli media doesn't want to check if this is a coincidence or if the judiciary is being exploited to turn around some election results.

Meanwhile, under enormous public pressure, the Shabak agitator Avishai Raviv, who was used by the Leftist political establishment to secure support for then PM Yitzhak Rabin, was finally indicted... sort of. He will have to face trial, but not for incitement to murder, instead for not doing enough to prevent a murder. As pathetic an indictment as it was, the judiciary put off the trial until July 6, well after Barak is safely in power.

Must I add that coverage of Raviv's indictment was a one-day, perfunctory affair instead of the continuing front-page story it deserved to be? Which brings up another two-word phrase the media and all political parties have not raised, even once.

3. Rabin Assassination: If Rabin was actually murdered by a right wing fanatic, Labor and Meretz would be running amok blaming the Right for the act. But they know that was not the case, and they also know Likud will pull out all stops releasing the facts if the Left dares to exploit Rabin's demise in its campaign for parliament. So there is no mention of the assassination in the media whatsoever, and sadly, I am a victim of this hush-up.

The biggest secret the media is withholding is that the Hebrew version of my book *Who Murdered Yitzhak Rabin* is a runaway bestseller in its first week on sale. I received the following information, and I trust the source:

The book is causing profound consternation in the Labor/Meretz camp, since it exposes and names the folks behind the murder as coming from this camp. A 1/3 page ad for the book placed by its publisher Gefen Books in *Ha'aretz* was the last straw. The Rabin family itself sent out word that the media will not touch the book, discuss its contents or ever mention my name in print or electronically, ideally forever. High-ranking politicians and military officers were recruited to instill this message with editors and producers. There was no problem convincing them, lest this book of mine influence Barak's chances for victory.

This election is one huge media manipulation, characterized not by what it is reporting, as by what it is not. And that's just the way Barak likes it.

THE PLOTTERS ARE BACK

While the election campaign dragged on, two events that could have changed the results occurred but they were not allowed to make a difference. On March 10, a group of twenty citizens submitted over 30 pieces of evidence to Tel Aviv Police and requested a reopening of the Rabin assassination investigation based on undeniable medical and police laboratory findings proving Yigal Amir could not have shot fatal bullets at Yitzhak Rabin.

Then, on April 29, my book *Who Murdered Yitzhak Rabin* was released in Hebrew by Gefen Books of Jerusalem. Within were the same documents submitted to the police the month before. What follows is a partial list of reporters who recognized the importance of the events and began preparing reports:

Yehudit Yeheskieli- *Yediot Ahronot*
Pearly Shahar- Channel One News
Immanuel Halperin- Channel One News
Sheike Rosenblat- Radio Kol Chai
Dror Skornick- *Makor Rishon*
Limor Shmuel- *Yerushalayim*

In each and every case, their editors and producers nixed their stories. The public was not permitted to hear the truth about the Rabin assassination and when that same public went to the polls today, they did not have the facts. If they did, the vote would have been different, one would hope, because no one would willingly place murderers in power...one would prefer to believe.

Though you wouldn't know it by the media blackout, thousands of Israelis have read my book in Hebrew and Russian in the past two weeks. People contacted me to say they had decided to change their vote after reading the book, and had the book received the exposure it warranted, there would have been many others. However, powerful forces made sure the public was not exposed to what should have been the central issue of the campaign—the conduct of the previous Labor government and its role in the Rabin assassination.

Not a few readers have commented that the reign of terror imposed on opponents of the Oslo Accords, and then the Rabin assassination could not possibly have taken place without the direct knowledge and connivance of Labor Party leader Shimon Peres and IDF Chief of

Staff Ehud Barak. As obvious as this is to my readers, I have never publicly commented on this observation.

As if this will do the truth any good. Aside from the new Prime Minister Ehud Barak, as number two on the Labor list, Shimon Peres will probably be a cabinet minister. And they will repress investigation of the Rabin murder with all the power they possess, and that is much, much greater than they had in the past three years when a few brave researchers were allowed to demand justice based on their indisputable proofs of high level official involvement in the Rabin murder and the incitement which preceded it.

One of these people is journalist Adir Zik, who told me, "This time round they aren't going to make the same mistakes. If anyone gets in their way they will be arrested even if it means setting up detention camps to hold them all."

It might not be a bad idea to get a copy of *Who Murdered Yitzhak Rabin* before the ax falls on it and me. I am preparing myself for an attack of some kind against my book. If the last time around is a good precedent, a full-frontal vicious media slander campaign will be followed by righteous violence. Anyone too vocal or visual in his indignation against the sellout of his nation should expect the same, and should not be surprised by how far they are willing to go to get their way.

They're back. *Oy Vavoy Lanu.*

CHAPTER 3

GOING... GOING... GOLAN

SECRETS OF THE GOLAN

In January 1996, the business magazine section of the Tel Aviv-based daily newspaper *Globes* published a two part series revealing a profoundly important fact that was unexplainably ignored: Israel has legal title over a large chunk of the Golan Heights and Western Syria.

In the 1890s, Baron Rothschild purchased 20,000 acres of Syrian land owned by the Ottoman Empire. In 1942, the Syrian government illegally confiscated the land. The Baron transferred the deeds to the Jewish National Fund (JNF) in 1957. In 1992, the deeds were moved to the Prime Minister's Office where they are stored today.

After I read the series, I called a contact in the JNF, Bunny Alexandroni of the public relations department. She said she'd look into the matter, and called me back. She informed me that she couldn't comment on the *Globes* series but asked me to meet her at her office. An appointment was made and she told me that her boss, the director of her department, would talk to me if I agreed not to publish his name.

After so agreeing, I entered his office and he invited me to be seated. He explained,

> "The *Globes* articles were essentially correct. They were a bit off on the location of the Rothschild land. Some of it is in the Golan but most is in the Horan, in Syria itself. I informed the government that the deeds are an excellent bargaining chip with the Syrians but the government refuses to play it. My hands are tied. I've been instructed not to pursue the matter."

And that is the biggest secret of the Golan: the Israeli government is holding onto legal title to land in the Golan and beyond and is hiding the fact from the public. Of course, the first question would be, why?

What follows is a chronological explanation of how the current Israeli-Syrian "peace" talks came to be. For those who are unable to dramatically readjust their sense of reality, it is advised to simply stop reading and make do with the knowledge of the land titles. They are more than enough to assure that Israel remains atop the Golan Heights. For those willing to accept a drastic switch in point of view, keep reading.

December 1990 - President George Bush invites Syria to join his coalition of forces to fight Iraq. The only offer Syria will respond to is a promise that America will use its power to remove Israel from the Golan Heights. Bush's administration has already secretly transferred $5.5 billion to Iraqi dictator Saddam Hussein and is in constant contact with him. Before the first shot of the Persian Gulf War is fired, Hussein agrees to bombard Israel with Scud missiles. In return, he is promised that no matter what the outcome of the war, he will not be brought down, nor will Israel respond to the attacks.

Bush promises Syria a bombardment that will prove to the Israeli people that territory will not protect them in the age of missiles. Later America will put the squeeze on the Shamir government to relinquish the Heights. Syria accepts the terms and joins the coalition.

Summer 1991 - Bush organizes a conference in Madrid to put international pressure on the Shamir government to leave the Golan. Shamir refuses to budge. Bush meets Syrian President Assad in Geneva. There, Assad says he's running out of patience with Bush and threatens to take matters into his own hands before the upcoming American elections. Bush promises that he will use all his power to remove Shamir from office and bring in a more compliant government.

June 23, 1992 - Bush's strategy of withholding loan guarantees and demonizing Shamir succeeds and Yitzhak Rabin becomes Israeli Prime Minister. Bush demands an immediate Golan withdrawal and Rabin explains that it is politically out of the question for him.

September 10, 1992 - Foreign Minister Shimon Peres meets French President Mitterand and Foreign Minister Roland Dumas in Paris and agrees to promote a total Golan withdrawal. He wants to meet with Syrian FM Farouk Shara immediately. Peres returns to Israel and Rabin meets him at Ben Gurion Airport. He orders Peres to stay away from the French, loudly calling them "the biggest bastards."

Too late for Rabin. Two days later Dumas begins a shuttle between Damascus and Cairo to coordinate Peres' Golan withdrawal.

September 17, 1992 - Rabin is called to Kennebunkport, Maine where an agitated Bush lays down the law. He must neutralize Peres' French track and "prepare the Israeli people for painful withdrawals," first from the Golan and then the West Bank and Gaza. He demands that the Golan withdrawal be coordinated with a compliant military leader, IDF Chief of Staff Ehud Barak. Rabin returns to Israel and announces his Syria First peace program.

September 23, 1993 - Syria is put on the back burner by the new Clinton administration, while negotiations with the PLO are taking place. Once Rabin inks a deal with Arafat, the White House begins its campaign for a Golan treaty. A meeting is set up between Chief of Staff Ehud Barak and VP Al Gore to get the track going.

November 12, 1993 - An international race is on to see who can get Israel off the Golan first. On the same day that Rabin is in Washington, accompanied secretly by Ariel Sharon, Peres is in France meeting with his French counterpart Alain Juppe. The Washington meetings go badly. The biggest sticking point is Syria's demand that as part of a peace deal, Israel give up its nuclear weapons program. While Rabin and Sharon refuse to accede, Peres shows no such compunctions.

December 6, 1993 - Secretary of State Warren Christopher flies to Damascus for a meeting with Syrian VP Hassan Habibi and most telling, with Jordanian Hamas leader Ibrahim Rusha. Syria lays down the law. The French have made a better offer and unless America moves Rabin in the same direction, Syria will promote a Hamas overthrow of the PLO regime in Gaza and the West Bank. Syria offers Hamas' violent talents for a terror campaign to remove Rabin from power in favor of Peres. Christopher relays the threats to Clinton and a summit between Assad and the American president is arranged for the following month.

January 1994 - Clinton and Assad meet in Geneva. Arafat, apprised of the plot against him, rushes to Geneva where the Swiss authorities refuse to grant him an entrance visa. Clinton promises

Assad a total Golan retreat and Rabin reacts with furor. He announces that any Golan deal would now be subject to a public referendum and appoints his Deputy Defense Minister, Motta Gur, to introduce a referendum bill in the Knesset.

May 1994 - Peres orders his Foreign Ministry staff to prepare a plan for the evacuation of Jewish residents of the Golan and presents it to Mitterand with a request for an immediate meeting with the Syrians. The Syrians now want Rabin out and Peres in and plan a strategy to achieve the goal.

July 1994 - Assad finally takes matters in his own hands and orders the bombing of the Israeli embassy in Buenos Aires. Over a hundred Jews die. Syria's responsibility is traced conclusively by two Argentinian journalists. The suicide bomb vehicle is rented with currency traced to Damascus. Rabin is ordered by his American bosses to cover up Syria's role in the atrocity and Israel shifts blame to Iran.

October 17, 1994 - The repercussions of Buenos Aires do not budge Rabin, so Syria orders a strike closer to home. A bus explodes in Tel Aviv killing 23. The same day, a Palestinian radio station in Damascus gives full details of the blast's methodology, two days before Israel police confirmed the accuracy of the report.

November 1994 - With Syria living up to its threats to remove Rabin, Clinton initiates a Damascus-Jerusalem shuttle. Rather than softened by the slaughter of Jews, Rabin was furious and his position on Syria hardened. Clinton finally relents and agrees to replace Rabin with a more compliant candidate—Ehud Barak.

December 1994 - Peres takes a major step towards realizing his Golan plan and invites Germany and Japan to place troops on the Heights after withdrawal goes into effect.

January 1995 - Ehud Barak quits his post as Chief of Staff. A month later he meets with Warren Christopher in Jerusalem to plan his future.

March - June 1995 - Barak flies to Washington and immediately begins negotiations with the Syrian peace-talks delegation. He promises a total Golan withdrawal if he becomes Prime Minister. He spends the rest of his trip planning his accession to power and understanding his role as envisioned by the Council on Foreign Relations. He holds meetings with CFR executives Henry Kissinger, Lawrence Tisch and. Edgar Bronfman. They vow to finance his campaign. Barak announces that the triumvirate agreed to finance his new "business" career to the tune of $30 million.

July 1995 - Barak returns to Israel and Rabin appoints him Interior Minister. Motta Gur is dead, supposedly of a suicide caused by depression over his cancer. His physician says that can't be; his disease was in total regression and he had everything to live for.

October 20, 1995 - The CFR has gotten wind of a French plot to murder Rabin and replace him with Peres. They decide to give Rabin a last chance. At the UN's 50th anniversary ceremony, Christopher and special advisor Dennis Ross remind Rabin that he promised a withdrawal to the shores of Lake Kinneret. They want him to meet with Shara and live up to his commitment. Rabin loses his cool and lets loose a loud and ugly rant against both of them. He shouts that he made the Kinneret comment sarcastically and they knew it. He threatens to pull out of the whole peace process. One by one, CFR members like Bronfman, Kissinger and Clinton try to sway Rabin. He gives his answer on the UN podium the next day, telling the assembled that he comes from Jerusalem, the undivided capital of Israel and that the real problem in his region wasn't Israel's stubbornness, it was Arab terrorism. The next day he flew to Washington and oversaw the passage of two congressional bills, which effectively neutralized the Oslo process. One bill declared that Jerusalem would never be divided, the other cut off American aid to the PLO if it declared a state. The Americans decided to keep Rabin ignorant of the French plot against him. Peres had to be next in line anyway before Barak could replace him.

November 7, 1995 - The leaders of the Anglo-American and European regimes descend on Rabin's funeral. With Rabin safely entombed, the squeeze begins to neutralize the French victory. John Major and Prince Charles arrange a meeting at Orient House for Peres to negotiate directly with Assad by phone. He turns the meeting down. However, he did promise Clinton an immediate withdrawal from the South Lebanon security zone and without an ounce of sentiment for Rabin's mourning period, the president sends Ross shuttling between Assad and Peres. Assad turns down Peres' limited offer and Clinton demands a major concession: Peres agrees to appoint his bitter rival, Barak, as his Foreign Minister and campaign manager for the next national elections.

January 1996 - Rabin's most precious Golan secret is leaked in detail to the business newspaper *Globes*. Israel had legal title to 20,000 acres of Syrian territory, some of it on the Golan Heights. The media is instructed to bury the story.

February - May 1996 - Barak and the Americans sabotage Peres' election campaign through a combination of deliberate incompetence, suicide bombers and a mini-war in Lebanon that costs Peres the Arab vote. Peres loses, and millions of dollars are funneled to Barak's successful campaign to take over the leadership of the Labor Party. The price was Netanyahu's victory, and immediately a campaign of scandal mongering begins to force him from power. Netanyahu survives the scandals, and freezes the Golan withdrawal, until the Americans invest their money and talents to assuring Barak's election in May 1999.

November 1999 - On the fourth anniversary of Rabin's murder, the public demands to know how he really died. Indisputable proof that the convicted assassin could not have shot the fatal bullets was in the hands of tens of thousands of people. My book with the documents within is number three on the bestseller list. Rabin's wife and two children demand a new investigation of his assassination. 65% of the public support their demand. A huge issue was needed to quell the fast-spreading public campaign to reinvestigate Rabin's demise. The truth would explode the whole peace process and incriminate the current leadership in atrocious crimes. A replacement murder scandal involving publisher Ophir Nimrodi works for a week but something far more lasting and devastating was required. An impending withdrawal from the Golan Heights does the trick.

WHY THE GOLAN SQUEEZE?

My explanation of the Anglo-American/French race to be the first to force Israel off the strategically vital Golan Heights, which ultimately led to the Rabin assassination, was widely accepted. I was gratified to see the piece translated into Hebrew within two days and then widely disseminated in Israel through major Internet sites, including that of the Golan residents themselves.

However, many readers were left with one question that I did not answer: why is there such an international push to pressure Israel off the Heights and thus leave its northern flank exposed to a relatively easy attack?

The most important explanation, by far, follows.

Let us begin with an event that occurred this week and is less distantly relevant than one might think. A few days ago, Regional Affairs Minister Shimon Peres was the driving force behind an agreement between Egypt and Israel to build a natural gas pipeline over the Sinai to supply a high percentage his country's future energy requirements. The chief financial benefactor was an engineering company with long-term ties to Peres called Merhav, and that is no coincidence since Peres has a strong attachment to pipelines.

In 1985 Iran blockaded the Persian Gulf and Iraq could not transport its oil exports by ship. At the same time, Syria blocked its overland route to the Mediterranean. Since 80% of Iraq's GNP came from its oil exports, the situation was dire, costing the Iraqis some $80 billion annually. To overcome the Iran/Syrian chokehold, Iraq sought to build a pipeline to the Jordanian Red Sea port of Aqaba. The Bechtel Corporation in America was contracted to construct the multi-billion dollar project but would not take the risk unless the pipe would remain secure even in war.

So Bechtel contacted Attorney-General Edwin Meese to bribe Prime Minister Shimon Peres. Eventually, Peres agreed to sign an agreement committing Israel never to attack the pipeline, even in a war against Jordan or Iraq. The price was a generous $70 million a year for ten years, to be deposited in the accounts of the Israeli Labor Party. When word of this expensive insurance policy cum bribe was leaked in Washington, Meese was forced to resign as Attorney General. But, as usual, in Israel, scandal escaped Peres.

With this pipeline blocked, Iraq still found itself totally dependent on Syria and Iran to secure safe passage for its oil. But there was an alternative route, and a most practical and lucrative one at that. However, ultimately it could only be opened if Israel left the Golan Heights for good. Within six years, Iraq was launching SCUD missiles at Israel to this end.

Still, the Iraqis are just a minor element in the Golan squeeze. The major elements are the Bechtel Corporation and the French government.

First Bechtel. This is a huge engineering corporation that long ago decided that its most profitable strategy was to combine earnings with global politics. In order to secure the lushest building contracts the world had to offer, it was deemed essential that the American government have free access to any part of the globe where leaders could be compromised and natural resources could be looted. Thus Bechtel has always been a vocal supporter of the rubric "free trade," which in essence means American and European corporations are free to drive local companies out of business worldwide. For the first half-century, Bechtel VP Cordell Hull was assigned the task of selling first the League of Nations and then the UN to the American people. Needless to say, his unfortunate legacy lives on.

As does Bechtel influence over American foreign policy. The means to this end is a 3000 member think tank in Manhattan called the Council on Foreign Relations (CFR), which has sent the majority of Presidents and Secretaries of State to Washington for the past two generations. Some recent examples: Caspar Weinberger was a VP at the Bechtel Power Corporation, while George Schultz served for a time as president of the company. When Bechtel is short of executives to directly run American policy, it recruits others with promises of wealth. For instance, when Henry Kissinger left public service for the private sector, Bechtel became one his first and most munificent clients.

Now we step back in time to the Cordell Hull era. In 1917, British forces overcame the Ottoman Turks and took over their empire. In 1923, the British divvied up the Middle East, giving its ally the French some leftovers. After surveying Syria and finding oil only in the northern Mosul region, Britain ceded the "worthless" Golan Heights to the French. Had they employed some geological foresight, the Brits would have been far more reluctant to give away such a valuable prize.

We jump to 1942 and with the prompting of Hull and Bechtel, Roosevelt draws America into World War Two. It takes a lot of oil to win a war, and for the past decade American and European surveyors had discovered that as much as half the world's reserves were buried under the sands surrounding the Persian Gulf, with the lion's share situated in Saudi Arabia. With the Nazis threatening the Suez Canal and supertankers unthought of, getting this oil to the Allies in Europe was a risky business in the extreme.

But Hull had a solution: build a Trans-Arabian pipeline from the Gulf to the Mediterranean and half the world's oil would flow cheaply and securely to Europe. And who better to build the pipe than his own company, Bechtel? With unusual haste, even for wartime, ARAMCO hired Bechtel to build the pipe.

There was one obstacle in the way of complete control over the flow of Gulf oil: the French. To get the oil to the Mediterranean, the ideal route was to the Golan Heights and then gravitationally to sea level. However, the French had legal hegemony over the Golan and ARAMCO and Bechtel had no choice but to cut them in on the profits. This agreement was upheld as part and parcel of the French departure from Syria in 1946, the very year when the pipeline was finished.

Then came the Six Day War of 1967, which saw Israel liberate the Golan Heights and the Arab states shut off the tap to the pipeline until the day when no more Jews set foot on the land. Initially American policy took advantage of Israel's hold on the newly won Suez Canal and Golan Heights by profiting heavily in the supertanker business, but the long-term policy was to get Israel out of both spots, no matter what her security concerns. Bechtel's CFR member, Weinberger arranged Meese's bribe to Peres under President Reagan, while President Bush's Bechtel CFR member George Schultz was charged with getting Israel out of the Golan. I have already detailed how the Persian Gulf War was created with this in mind. In short, Syria joined the Bush fighting coalition in return for a promise that America would press Israel off the Golan, while Iraq softened the country up with missile attacks, proving territory means little in the age of SCUDS.

With Israeli Prime Minister Shamir refusing to budge on Bush's postwar Golan withdrawal demands, Bush used all the powers of his government to oust him and replace him with a more compliant client, Yitzhak Rabin. Yet Rabin's rise to power was also a windfall for the French, whose long-term factotum Shimon Peres was now second in command as Foreign Minister. By September of 1992, Peres had promised the French that he would arrange Israel's descent from the

Heights. This promise spurred a shuttle between Cairo and Damascus by French Foreign Minister Roland Dumas, much to the open disgust of Rabin.

I described the race between the French and Anglo-Americans to get Israel off the Golan Heights, but I did not state that the primary reason was to get the Bechtel oil flowing from the Saudi, Gulf and Iraqi fields to the Mediterranean. This is not a minor diplomatic consideration: with Gulf oil flowing undeterred to the Mediterranean, those with their fingers on the nozzles would be in a position to undercut, thus control, the world's petroleum supply.

There are no Israeli heroes in the sad sellout of the Golan but it must be remarked that Rabin displayed great courage in holding out for a compromise that would have left Israeli troops in place on a strategic axis of the Heights. That cost him his life. With Peres willing to sell out every inch of Israel's northern security, the French decided to earn their percentage of the Trans-Arabian Pipeline profits by placing him in power. Unfortunately for them, a bungled assassination has been exposed and it is threatening not merely their cut of the oil profits, but the political future of Peres and of the entire Labor Zionist movement. A cutthroat cover-up is taking place in Israel to save the plotters but it is relentlessly crumbling.

Did the French act alone to remove Rabin? So far the trail to France is overwhelming. To name but two connections, the head of the Israeli secret services, Carmi Gillon, was in Paris the night of the murder and the fatal rally where Rabin fell was organized and paid for by Peres' French ally, the media tycoon Jean Frydman. But one must not forget that Bechtel and the Americans benefited greatly by the sudden departure of the recalcitrant Rabin, and by the eventual ascendancy of their client Ehud Barak. At a minimum, the evidence so far indicates that they did not stand in the way of the murder.

Rabin refused to budge for Bechtel and he had to go. Now no Israeli political leader stands in the way of the secret sellout of the Golan Heights.

THE FORMULA FOR DISASTER

KOSOVO - LAST STOP BEFORE JERUSALEM

Barely a few days before the EU and the US, collectively called NATO, sent their flying dogs of war against Serbia, Israeli Prime Minister Binyamin Netanyahu was in Berlin meeting with the leaders of the European Union. You would think with the attack on the Balkans pending they'd be too busy to have time for a little tete-a-tete with Bibi...But, no; they organized their most fateful meeting with an Israeli leader since the beginning of their continental unity. They told him he'd better not stand in the way of a PLO state with East Jerusalem as its capital or watch out.

The watch out part was Kosovo.

Netanyahu got the message and like the Yugoslav president Milosevic before him, flew to Russia for some counterweight. And lo and behold, the Kremlin greeted him like visiting royalty. When the meetings were over, Bibi and Boris agreed to make a united stand against "Islamic fanaticism." What they meant to say, but could not, was that both Israel and Russia were sick of the New World Order plots against their nations and they were forming a—probably futile—little alliance against the Trilateral Commission, Council on Foreign Relations (CFR), Bilberberg group and all those who were now heating up the Balkans, and Chechnya, and Turkey and everywhere else where ethnic tensions could be turned into massacres.

Undoubtedly, both leaders are well aware of how it's done. Take a busload of Christian Lebanese children, blow it up, blame it on the PLO and before long you've got perfectly civilized Christians killing Moslems out of raw bloodlust. Or take a Serb village, more if necessary, have some Bosnian Muslims kill every living being within and before long, you'll get just the right kind of savagery from the Serbs.

Then you make the Lebanese Christians the bad guys with a stage-managed media campaign portraying them as bloodthirsty fascists determined to wipe out the hapless, innocent Palestinians who tried to carve out their own fiefdom out of Lebanon. Apply the same formula to Kurds, Tutsis, Israelis, Afrikaaners and Serbs. The important thing is to back Marxist Moslems over democratic Christians and Jews. And once the world has been indoctrinated enough to think there is an issue of right and wrong to be dealt with, send in the planes followed by the ground troops of the New World Order armed services.

And once the white Christians and Jews are out of power in Africa, it becomes so much easier to take control of the wealth and resources of a whole continent. All you have to do is install more Marxist dictators, stir up wars, spread epidemics of incurable diseases and now you're talking real easy pickings.

Around 1992, the CFR decided to begin a campaign of worldwide "peace processes" all formulated to result in ghastly wars. After manipulating the fall of the Soviet Union a few years before, innumerable opportunities awaited them behind the former Iron Curtain. After such NWO personalities as Henry Kissinger and Lord Carrington eliminated the last bastions of wealth and security in Africa, it was a piece of cake for them to initiate bloodbaths in Somalia and Rwanda. Soon the NWO planners will turn their attentions to other "peace processes" they started in Northern Ireland and Israel, but first they must dispose of Yugoslavia.

It all began around 1990 when the CFR sent Kissinger Associates partner Lawrence Eagleburger to Belgrade to corrupt and worm his way into the Yugoslav leadership. He bought a controlling interest in the country's largest bank for his bosses, he even introduced the Yugo car to America, bankrolling a large chain of dealerships.

Once the ruling classes were corrupted, the standard methods were employed to stir ethnic rivalries and force the Serbian hand. As usual, peoples who had drifted to historical Serb lands to seek improved economic opportunities were propagandized and heated up enough to declare their desire for independent breakaway states. This, no sovereign nation could tolerate and like the Russians in Chechnya or the Israelis in Jerusalem, the governments had no choice but to draw the line to save the souls of their nations.

So, armed and organized challenges to the government had to be funded. And like the PLO, Afghanis, half a dozen Latin American rebel groups before them, etc., etc. the European drug trade was opened to the Kosovo Liberation Army. Today NATO is fighting on behalf of one of the largest heroin suppliers of Western Europe. But that's par for the NWO course.

32

Once the fighting began, in came the NWO "peacemakers": Vance, Christopher, Holbrooke, Albright, every one of them a loyal CFR member, to impose conditions the Serbs could never possibly accept. Milosevic's unforgivable crime was standing up to the NWO and refusing to allow its army to roam his land at will.

And for this he is being punished. And Netanyahu has got the message. If he doesn't play ball, he will be demonized just like Milosevic, the world will be primed to despise him and in will come the NWO's air force. If he doesn't give the PLO its state on historical Jewish territory this year, here is what will happen:

The PLO will unilaterally declare a state and Israel will annex the remaining West Bank territories in her possession. A wave of Arab terrorism will force Israel to retaliate and a cycle of violence will begin which will duplicate that of Yugoslavia. The "peacemakers" of the NWO will arrive and insist that Israel accept every clause of the Oslo Accords, give up its history and heritage to the PLO and divide Jerusalem. When Israel refuses to relent, it will be painted quickly as a mortal danger to the peace of the planet. In order to "save" Israel from itself, the NWO forces will attack and impose its solutions on her.

And to most of the world, the events that lead to this war will seem totally logical. Like, in Kosovo today, the media will stage-manage every step of the war and a world under televised anesthesia will believe the broadcasters, generals and military experts. And this world will simply sleep through Israel's destruction. When it awakes it will change channels.

THE NON-JEWS BEHIND KOSOVO

The American team behind the Yugoslav War have Jewish names and look very Jewish. This is a sad and humiliating fact...and it shouldn't take the anti-semites long to make a few associations and call the bloodletting in the Balkans a Jewish plot. However, if a plot exists, it is being managed by the very antithesis of Judaism, those who have abandoned Judaism for good.

Let us look at the core of the visible team:

* William Cohen—Secretary of Defense—Longtime member of the Council on Foreign Relations. Headed the notorious 1997 CFR Task Force on the Middle East, which called for Israel's withdrawal to 1948 lines and the division of Jerusalem, until replaced later by Henry Seigman. Though he has a Jewish father, Cohen was raised as Protestant and maintains no Jewish religious ties whatsoever.

* Mad Madeleine Albright—Secretary of State—Longtime member of the CFR. Her story is absolutely surreal. Born and raised Jewish in Czechoslovakia, she escaped the Holocaust and was cared for by Jewish relatives in London. Yet, over the years she forgot her entire childhood and adolescence, claiming she's always been a Christian. Her memory was jarred only when *The Washington Post* printed her true biography during the very week she was appointed Secretary of State. The woman did not simply disavow her Jewish roots, for fifty years she pretended they didn't exist. And for much of her term in office, she has been obsessed with pressing Israel to withdraw to suicidal borders.

* James Rubin—State Department Spokesman—Member of the CFR. Recently married CNN Kosovo reporter Christiane Amanpour in a church. Claims to have adopted Christianity. While longtime CFR member Ted Turner's CNN grinds out the New World Order vision through Amanpour, Rubin coordinates the illusion as Albright's supercilious mouthpiece.

This trio is hiding behind the bloodshed they are fomenting with a curtain woven of humanitarian goodness for the Kosovo refugees. Never mind that the refugees would not have been there to cover their deeds without the NATO bombing of Yugoslavia. So far the facade is holding up but the curtain will eventually fall and when it does, thanks to this triumvirate of evil, Jews are going to be left holding the bag.

When that day comes, let all so inclined to see the Jewish hand in NWO machinations recall that this war is in the hands of people who found the deep morality of Judaism not to their liking. They abandoned Judaism, and while Yugoslavia is their current target for destruction, Israel is next on their list.

CHAPTER 5

WHO KILLED COCK RABIN?

EXPOSING THE RABIN ASSASSINATION TRUTH

It took two years before Americans began to suspect that Lee Harvey Oswald did not shoot President Kennedy. It took large sections of the Israeli population less than a week to suspect that Yigal Amir did not shoot the fatal bullets at Prime Minister Yitzhak Rabin. It took me about two hours. At about midnight of November 4, 1995, I asked how Amir could possibly have broken through Rabin's bodyguards to take a clear shot at Rabin's back. My answer was that he couldn't have... unless someone wanted him to.

The next day my suspicions were reinforced by eye-witness testimonies that appeared in the media. After Amir's first shot, one witness after another heard Rabin's bodyguards shout, "They're blanks," "They're not real," and the like. And then, instead of killing Amir on the spot, the same bodyguards let him get off two more rounds. It just didn't add up. The bodyguards are trained to shoot an assassin in less than a second; it would take longer to shout, "They're blanks, they're not real." Why would they think the bullets were duds? Why didn't they kill Amir to save Rabin?

And far more seriously, why did they allow Amir into the so-called sterile security area where only authorized personnel were permitted entrance? The next day, Israel TV broadcast a film clip of Amir being taken away from an anti-Rabin demonstration just two weeks before. Amir was well known to Rabin's security detail; he was a member of the most extreme anti-Rabin right wing organization of all, Eyal, an acronym for Jewish Warriors, run by the most extreme right wing radical of them all, the notorious Avishai Raviv.

On November 10, a public accusation was made by (now) Knesset Member Benny Elon that Avishai Raviv was in fact an agent for the General Security Services (Shabak), the very same Shabak charged with protecting Rabin. If people scoffed, it was only for a day. On November 11, a respected left wing journalist Amnon Abramovich broke the truth on Israel's Television One: Raviv was a Shabak officer code-named Champagne, whose duty was to infiltrate groups opposed to the government's peace process and incriminate them. To make his task easier, he created a straw group called Eyal and hyper-radicalized young people, turning legitimate protest into illegitimate outrages. He was the Shabak's chief provocateur.

From that moment on, it was a matter of time before the conspiracy to assassinate Rabin was exposed. The assassin belonged to an organization created by the very Shabak that was charged with protecting Rabin. And that was not all. Amir had spent the spring and summer of 1992 in Riga, Latvia working with a nest of spies called the Prime Minister's Liaison Office, or Nativ for short. There, the newspapers reported, he had received training from the Shabak.

Yigal Amir was not just a religious kid who got mad one night and shot a Prime Minister. He had an intelligence background.

Enter the First Informer

At the time, I was the co-editor of Israel's only intelligence newsletter, called *Inside Israel*. My partner was Joel Bainerman. We had both written books, recently published. My book, *The Fall of Israel* (Cannongate Publishers, Edinburgh) was about political corruption; his book *Crimes of a President* (SPI Books, New York) was about the covert and illegal operations that took place during the Bush administration. Combined, we were producing the most honest reporting of Israel's hidden political shenanigans anywhere. We had gained a strong reputation in numerous circles for the exposés of the criminal deceit that lay behind Israel's agreements with the PLO.

And that is why one Moshe Pavlov chose to call me on November 17. His first call was brief: "Watch Channel Two News tonight and you'll see me," he said. "Then I'll call back." He appeared on the news and was described as one of the country's most dangerous right wing leaders. Odd, I thought, why hadn't I heard of him before?

The next call wasn't from Pavlov but from my neighbor Joel Bainerman. Though he lived in a most obscure location, Pavlov found his way to Joel's doorstep and appeared unannounced. Joel said, "I don't think we should meet here. I'll see you downtown in ten minutes."

Though he aggressively denies it, all, literally all my sources later told me Pavlov is a Shabak agent. In retrospect, there is no other way he could have had the information in his possession if he wasn't an insider. Joel and I sat in a quiet corner of the town square of Bet

Shemesh, as a terrified and agitated Moshe Pavlov spewed out reams of—what turned out to be—the truth.

"Amir was supposed to shoot blanks," he insisted. "That's why the bodyguards shouted that he did. He was supposed to. It was a fake assassination. Rabin was supposed to survive the blank bullets, dramatically go back on the podium, condemn the violence of his opponents and become a hero. That's how he was going to save the Oslo Accords. Raviv was supposed to give him the gun with the blanks but Amir got wind of the plan and changed the bullets."

Pavlov was way off on this point. Later evidence proved beyond doubt that Amir did shoot blanks and Rabin was shot elsewhere. Pavlov became nearly hysterical. "They're killing people to cover this up and they're setting me up for a fall. Already one of Rabin's bodyguards is dead."

He gave us the name of the bodyguard: Yoav Kuriel. He also supplied his details, including his social security number. A Yoav Kuriel was reported dead in the media the next day, but of a suicide. It would be another two years before I received his death certificate and spoke with the man who prepared his body for burial. He died of seven bullets to the chest. No one was allowed to identify his remains.

And then Pavlov gave us information that NO ONE was allowed to know. To this day, only the man's initials can legally appear in the Israeli media. "The guy behind the operation is Eli Barak, a lunatic. He runs the Shabak's Jewish Department. He is Raviv's superior and set up Amir to take the fall."

He added a fact that was positively unknown at the time. "Barak takes his orders from the head of the Shabak. His first name is Carmi, he lives in Mevasseret Tzion and that's all I want to say." It took over a year before the Israeli public was to learn the name of the Shabak Chief: Carmi Gillon.

Pavlov was insistent: "You have to publish this and my name. Otherwise I'm finished." Joel and I decided to publish the story in *Inside Israel*. When it came out, I met Pavlov at the Holiday Inn lobby in Jerusalem. We were surrounded by policemen. Wherever he went, they followed. That was good enough proof for me that our faith in Pavlov's version of events was justified.

An Assassination Film Emerges

Just under two months after the assassination, to the total shock of the nation, an "amateur" videotape of the murder emerged and it was broadcast over Channel Two. Joel taped the film from the television and we scrutinized it closely. Though we are being petty, to this day we argue over who caught the closing door first.

The story of Rabin's last two hours of life is bizarre now, as it was then. The drive to the hospital should have taken less than a minute. But the driver, Menachem Damti, claimed he became confused and that's why he got lost and took nine minutes to arrive. After seven minutes driving, he stopped the car and asked a cop, Pinchas Terem to get in the car and direct him to the hospital. So, only three people were supposed to be in the car until then, Rabin, the driver and the personal bodyguard Yoram Rubin.

In the film all three are clearly outside the vehicle, when the right back passenger door was slammed shut from the inside. There was a fourth person in the car waiting for Rabin.

We saw two other shocking moments. The first occurs just before Amir makes his move towards Rabin's back. Rabin's rear bodyguard stopped dead in his tracks, turned his head sideways and allowed the "killer" in. The act was deliberate, there was no doubting the film.

And then, after Amir shoots, Rabin turns his head in the direction of the shot and keeps walking...just like eye-witnesses said he did on the night of the assassination. Rabin was unhurt by Amir's shot to the back. It was a blank bullet after all.

A month later, the government-appointed Shamgar Commission of Inquiry into the Rabin Assassination issued its findings. It concluded that Amir shot twice at Rabin's back, once while Rabin was walking from 50 cm., then after he fell from about the same range. Very logical except the film showed that Amir never got anywhere near such close range for the second shot. In fact, he was no closer than six feet away for the second shot.

The contradictions had reached and far passed the point of being utterly ridiculous.

The Trial

After the government had already declared him the murderer, Amir stood trial for murder...which lets you know how fair a trial he received. Before the trial began, there was a hearing. When Amir stepped into the courtroom, he shouted to reporters:

"The whole system is rotten. If I open my mouth I can bring it all down. The people will forgive me when they know the truth. I didn't think they'd start killing anyone."

After this revealing outburst, he was taken away and never allowed to address journalists again. After a month in Shabak custody he appeared a different person for his trial: a grinning idiot determined to prove his own guilt. He had been transformed, we surmised by a combination of threats, promises, sleep deprivation and drugs.

The trial was barely covered by the media but what emerged was astounding. Damti and Rubin lied through their teeth. Just for starters, Damti claimed he was opening the door for Leah Rabin when the first shot rang out. Then he immediately sat in the driver's seat as he had been trained to do. The truth was that Leah Rabin was 24 feet away and nowhere in sight and the film showed that he did not sit in the driver's seat until Rabin was placed in the car.

And if those statements were mere whoppers, Rubin's version of events was a lollapalooza. He testified that he lay on top of Rabin and Rabin helped him get up. Then they both jumped headfirst into the car, Rabin landing on the seat, Rubin on the floor. Without elaborating on the depth of the lie, no witnesses saw Rabin jump and the film proves he didn't.

After the trial, I received my first prized secret document; the testimony of Chief Lieutenant Baruch Gladstein of the Israel Police Crime Laboratory, taken from the protocols of Amir's trial. After testing Rabin's clothes scientifically, Gladstein testified that the Prime Minister was shot from point blank, barrel on the skin, range. He insisted that his conclusion was certain and that the combination of massed gunpowder and an explosion tear on the clothing could only have occurred at 0 distance. Even half a centimeter would have been too far.

Amir never, ever shot from point blank range. He did not kill Rabin. That was enough for me. I gathered the film, and the testimonies and started giving lectures on the Rabin murder conspiracy in Jerusalem and the crowds who came to hear me were always large.

41

In October 1996, I received a phone call from the *Weekend Magazine* program of television Channel Two. They had heard about my lectures and also believed there were inconsistencies between the evidence and the Shamgar Commission findings. They wanted to interview me.

What liars they were! They broadcast an eight minute snow job that compared me to a Holocaust denier. And they rebroadcast the show the next night. At first it looked like a disaster for my life. The organizations which had sponsored my lectures were forced to cancel them, cabinet ministers condemned me as a "fascist" and a few threatening crank calls resulted.

However, the program did include the clip of Rabin's car door slamming shut when no one was supposed to be in the car. And a few of my strongest points slipped through loud and clear. People everywhere I went congratulated me on my courage. The show boomeranged and ended up encouraging me to carry on.

I was not the only one on the show. A Ramat Gan computer technician named Natan Gefen also appeared briefly with his own proofs. As a result of his appearance, the local Ramat Gan newspaper interviewed him at length about his evidence of a conspiracy behind the Rabin assassination.

One would not believe that Natan Gefen deserves to be recognized as one of the greatest investigators of all time. He doesn't look the part and by day he operates a computer at a pharmaceutical firm. But Gefen uncovered the most sensitive documents of any political assassination and here's how he did it.

He made a hundred copies of his interview in the Ramat Gan paper, added his fax number and a request for proof, and placed the document in every corner of the hospital Rabin was taken to, Ichilov. And someone faxed him Rabin's medical records.

What an incredible tale they told! The surgeon who operated on Rabin, Dr. Mordechai Gutman and his surgical team, recorded the following fact: Rabin arrived with two bullet holes in the back, was revived, was shot again and left with a third one in the front which passed through the upper lobe of his right lung and finally shattered dorsal vertebrae 5 and 6.

The conspiracy was broken. The State Pathologist's report erased all the wounds the hospital staff reported because Amir never shot from the front and couldn't have. And Rabin could not have had his backbone shattered because the videotape of the murder clearly shows him walking after the only shot to the upper back. Gefen had provided the definitive proof that Amir did not shoot the deadly bullets into Rabin.

I had to get the information out but my lectures were cancelled. Then Joel had a brilliant idea: if your lectures are cancelled, let's rent a hotel auditorium and do one ourselves. On a stormy January night in 1997, over 70 people braved the wet and arrived for the lecture. And Channel One television covered it.

I was back.

Attending the lecture was Brian Bunn, who sat on the Foreign Student's council of the Hebrew University of Jerusalem. He was impressed and booked me to speak at the country's most respected educational institute. This the Shabak could not tolerate, so they organized a violent riot against me. And I must thank them for that because I was front page news for a week in Israel, and the riot was covered worldwide.

Next, a smear campaign was organized against me in the Israeli media, but a few reporters listened to me, read the evidence I had gathered and wrote long, favorable pieces. And over 300 people contacted me within a week, ALL to congratulate me and some 20 to pass on invaluable information. I was invited to give the same lecture in New York, where I met Jay Sidman who set up a brilliant Rabin website for me at www.webseers.com/rabin. It turned into a meeting place for an international exchange of ideas and information about the assassination.

A Toronto lecture was videotaped and later sold commercially. I was really on that night and the videotape convinced tens of thousands of people that I was right. And best of all, the publicity led to book contracts, first in America, then in Israel and France. I took care with the book, reviews have been excellent and hundreds of thousands have been swayed by the facts.

In my follow-up book I may name the culprits: I know who did it. Right now, it's a bit too early for my fellow Jews and Israelis to digest the fact that Rabin was murdered from within his own political circle.

RABIN'S LAST DOCTOR

We now enter the realm of the truly bizarre as we look at the doctor who last examined Yitzhak Rabin, the State Pathologist Dr. Yehuda Hiss. Israelis know too well that their government's coroner is corrupt. In September 1999, Judge Ruth Orr overturned a conviction against a Jewish resident of Judea and Samaria for the shooting murder of an Arab boy because she accused Dr. Hiss of forging the forensic evidence against him. It was the second time in a year that a murder conviction was overturned because Hiss had falsified an autopsy for political purposes. He had earlier been caught doctoring the facts to secure a wrongful rap against the parents of a murdered child.

His biggest fabrication of all occurred after the country's most ghastly scandal was proven. In the first decade of Israel's existence, the Labor government kidnapped over 4500 babies, mainly of new Yemenite immigrant parents, and sold them off for adoption and medical experiments, mostly abroad. Through the efforts of Yemenite groups fighting to expose this crime, three years ago one mother, Margalit Omeisse, was reunited with her daughter Celia Levine, given up for adoption to a California couple almost half a century before. Besides looking like twins, the Hebrew University genetics laboratory proved they were mother and daughter by DNA testing. Dr. Hiss retested the two for the government and lo and behold, found that Hebrew University was wrong.

And that's why his nickname in certain circles is Dr. Cover-up.

People started calling him that about a year after the Rabin assassination. He conducted a partial autopsy of Rabin and concluded he was shot twice in the back from medium range. In 1996, Rabin's hospital records were uncovered and over ten doctors and nurses signed very different accounts of Rabin's demise. He was actually shot three times, twice from point blank range and once frontally in the upper chest. On top of that, Rabin's spine was shattered and Hiss categorically reported that it wasn't. Because the patsy Yigal Amir never shot from point blank range or from the front, and because the assassination film proved Rabin's spine could not have been broken since he kept right on walking after the shot to his back, somebody must have asked Hiss to alter the medical facts. So he did and then the government's commission of inquiry into the murder adopted Hiss's lies as the official version of Rabin's death.

So we knew that Hiss was corrupt and that he molded his reports to fit government orders. What we didn't know was that he is also genuinely ghoulish. Avi and Nitzana (Darshan) Leitner are Yigal Amir's attorneys. They also represent another victim of Dr. Hiss, the family of Alisdair Sinclair.

On April 14, 1998, 47 year old Alisdair Sinclair was stopped by customs officials at Ben Gurion Airport on his way out of the country after a six day stay. They found 9000 Deutsche marks in a false bottom of his handbag and he was arrested without charge. The police thought the false bottom suggested something illegal though hiding a large amount of money is a legitimate means of thwarting theft.

At the airport police station, Sinclair was found strangling on his shoelaces. He was rushed to a hospital and pronounced dead. From there his body was transferred to the Abu Kabir Institute for Forensic Medicine and straight into the paws of Dr. Yehuda Hiss, who conducted an autopsy which concluded that Sinclair had killed himself.

After that, there was a problem with the body. Sinclair was unmarried, his parents weren't alive and he had been living a rather rootless life in Amsterdam dealing in vintage guitars and strumming them at local pubs. It took three days to track down his family in Scotland and the police offered to bury him in Israel. The family refused and paid about $5000 to fly the corpse home.

On May 13, another autopsy was conducted, at the University of Glasgow and guess what? The hyoid bone at the base of the tongue was missing and so was the heart. Both were removed by Dr. Hiss. But why? No problem guessing why the hyoid bone was gone. It would reveal that Sinclair did not hang himself but was strangled by other means.

But the heart..? Avi Leitner can only say:

"Our best guess is that Hiss is involved in the black market trade in human organs. We can't prove that yet, but it seems the most likely motive for removing a healthy heart."

Incredibly, a most unlikely source provides an even spookier motive. But let's get on with the story first. The Sinclair family started investigating Alisdair's recent life and none of his friends thought him remotely suicidal. Nor did they understand why he was arrested for carrying perfectly legal currency in the first place. Israel police explained that they suspected he was a drug dealer and under interrogation he admitted to have smuggled in thousands of Ecstasy pills the week before, though he did not know who bought them. Alisdair's brother James, of Selkirk, Scotland, mocked the police version, noting accurately that since he wasn't caught with drugs, he had no reason whatsoever to confess to the supposed crime.

Enter the British government. Tel Aviv embassy official Suad Andraus was furious, stating, "People don't just die in lockup." The British authorities demanded that Dr. Hiss explain what he did with the heart and then return it immediately.

Hiss explained that as a drug smuggling suspect, the heart would have shown "signs of long-term drug abuse." Fine, so why didn't he return the heart with the rest of the body? According to Hiss: "It's true we didn't inform the family in Scotland that the heart was missing. Frankly, we didn't want to upset them."

How thoughtful, and returning the body without the heart wasn't in the least bit upsetting???? Hiss complied with the second demand and turned over the heart to the Sinclair family, or at least *a* heart. A not very convincing heart, at that. The Sinclair Family demanded DNA proof that this was Alisdair's heart but Dr. Hiss refused, citing the $6000 cost of the test. The Sinclairs found the cost prohibitive as well but this time, the British authorities did not press the issue or conduct their own tests.

A frustrated James Sinclair expressed his disgust with the inconsistencies of his brother's strange demise.

Alisdair never had a police record and it is unlikely that he would turn to drug smuggling. And he repeats, "Why would he admit to anything if his bloody suitcase was empty? My brother was an intelligent, well read man. He wasn't daft."

Currently, the Israeli Police are conducting DNA tests and James is awaiting the results, clearly unaware that if Dr. Yehuda "Cover-up" Hiss has his hands in the testing, the findings will be as honest as those of the Rabin assassination.

And now a most unexpected motive for the whole affair. It was published in *The Jerusalem Report*, a staid, establishment newsmagazine that is used as a fount of disinformation on behalf of the country's Labor Party. This peculiar passage may be of interest to those questioning Britain's early and deep interest in Zionism, their reverence for Chaim Weizman, the Balfour Declaration, the

British-Israel Society, the Round Table policies of Cecil Rhodes and Lord Milner and the like.

> "According to Alisdair's brother James, family lore has it that the Sinclairs are descended from the crusading Knights Templars, who journeyed to Jerusalem in the mid-1300s in search of holy artifacts from Herod's Temple to bring back to Scottish hero Robert Bruce. Alisdair himself, says James, was particularly proud of his middle name, Roslyn, the name of a chapel in Scotland whose floor plan is said to be based on Herod's Temple. James mentions these details in attempting to reconstruct his brother's motive for travelling to Israel."

How does this Medieval history explain Alisdair Sinclair's missing heart? Whether it does in some way or not, one thing is certain: The doctor who last examined Yitzhak Rabin is one very, weird sicko.

YIGAL "THE BEAV" AMIR TALKS TO JUNE WHILE *THE WASHINGTON POST* HAPPENED BY

[Editor's note: Interspersed within the following article are this author's comments, contained within the *{CURLY BRACES}*.]

Slayer Acknowledges Rabin's Cause Lives On
Assassin Favors Victim's Protege In Vote

By Laura Blumenfeld
Washington Post Staff Writer

Friday, May 14, 1999; Page A01

HERZLIYYA, Israel—The man who pumped three bullets into Prime Minister Yitzhak Rabin *{RABIN WAS SHOT TWICE ACCORDING TO THE SHAMGAR COMMISSION}* admitted this week that although he killed one of Israel's most famous peacemakers, he has failed to kill the peace process. *{DARN, THAT MUST BE DISAPPOINTING TO HIM}*

Yigal Amir, the 29-year-old religious extremist *{LET'S GET THAT DESCRIPTION IN EARLY}* who is serving a life sentence for Rabin's assassination, also said he favors Rabin's protege -- Labor party leader Ehud Barak -- in the upcoming elections. He joked that if elected, Barak might end up like Rabin. *{YUK YUK. GOOD LINE YIGAL}*

Banned from talking to journalists or anyone else outside his immediate family, Amir allowed a *Washington Post* reporter to listen in on a speaker phone conversation with his mother this week. *{MY, MY. HOW TIMELY. EXCUSE ME FOR SAYING SO, BUT MY BOOK MUST BE SCARING SOMEBODY. AMIR HASN'T BEEN QUOTED BY ANY NEWS AGENCY IN THREE YEARS}* He offered a rare glimpse of his life in deep isolation, days spent bent over holy texts on his concrete desk, answering fan mail from teenage girls, lathering up in a shower in front of 24-hour security cameras. *{AND HIS MOTHER NEEDS TO HEAR THIS?}*

His mother, Geula Amir, 49, talked to her son from his old room at the Amirs' white stucco home here, in a northern suburb of Tel Aviv.

48

He was 60 miles away at a prison in Beersheva, gripping a receiver handed through a slot in the metal door of his windowless chamber, where he is in solitary confinement.

Amir spoke to his mother in heavy, depressed tones, issuing sentences in rapid bursts. On Nov. 4, 1995, he fired a 9mm Beretta and thought he would change history forever; instead, the former law student got prison forever.

"Don't ask how I feel, and don't ask what I'm eating," he had told her in an earlier conversation. "If you ask me, I'll hang up." *{AH, THE STAGE IS SET.}* So this time his mother tried to direct the conversation to politics. "Who are you voting for?" she asked. *{(In Israel convicted felons are allowed to vote.) OF COURSE, THAT'S THE FIRST THING ON GEULA'S MIND. I WONDER WHAT THEY PROMISED HER TO PARTICIPATE IN THIS SHAM?}*

"I don't know. I wouldn't mind Barak," said Amir. "He's the same as [Prime Minister Binyamin] Netanyahu. Both are keeping the peace agreements, continuing on Rabin's path."

For Amir and other religious extremists in Israel, Netanyahu has proved to be a bitter disappointment. Amir has said he shot Rabin out of religious conviction, to prevent the return of the West Bank to the Palestinians. *{WHEN?? MOST OF AMIR'S STATEMENTS ARE IN MY BOOK. HOW DID I MISS THIS ONE?}* But Netanyahu has not prevented that return, and a Palestinian entity -- if not a state -- now exists on land formerly held by Israel.

Amir believes that Netanyahu is going out of his way to punish extreme right-wingers like himself, and that Netanyahu deserves to lose.

"You'll have better prison conditions if Barak is elected," said Geula Amir. *{SO THAT'S WHAT SHE WAS PROMISED.}*

"The left won't feel like they have anything to prove," Yigal added.

But he made it chillingly clear that he has not changed his views about the righteousness of his actions. According to Amir, a leader like Rabin, who forfeited land God gave exclusively to the Jews, deserved to die.

"You don't watch television," his mother said, "so you don't see it, but you would die laughing – Barak keeps showing these ads of him shaking hands with Rabin, standing next to Rabin, and he promises that he'll continue on Rabin's path." *{OKAY, WHO WROTE THE SCRIPT FOR GEULA?}*

"So let him follow Rabin," Yigal snickered. "Maybe he'll end up like him too." *{CHILLING TOUCH. I WONDER IF YIGAL HAD THE SCRIPT IN FRONT OF HIM?}* "Oh, shut up, you're disgusting," said Geula, scolding but affectionate. *{THE SCRIPTWRITER DIDN'T STUDY GEULA'S REAL SPEECH PATTERNS. SHE NEVER SPEAKS LIKE THIS. GEULA DOES NOT TAKE RABIN'S MURDER LIGHTLY AND WOULD NEVER SNICKER AT THIS PHONY ATTEMPT AT HUMOR.}*

These talks are part of the Amir family routine. Every day, between 6 and 7 p.m., a guard from the Beersheva prison in southern Israel calls on a special line that reverses the charges. After the guard confirms that the voice on the other end belongs to Amir's parents or to one of his seven siblings, he transfers the call. After 15 minutes, a bell rings, signaling the end of the conversation.

On this evening, Geula talked to her son from the room he used to live in.

Unlike the rest of the house, the walls in this room are fresh, and the windows new. After the assassination, police ripped the place apart, and discovered a cache of weapons.

"I don't know," she said. "I'm not sure what you did was worth it."

{SHE'S NOT SURE??????? AH, COME ON. THIS IS NO MOTHER-SON CONVERSATION AMONG HUMAN BEINGS, EXCEPT ON TV SITCOMS.}

Amir laughed bitterly. "You have no faith," he said. "If I hadn't [killed Rabin], there would have been a Palestinian state for a while already, no Jewish settlements, we would have lost everything."

"But there already is a Palestinian state," his mother said with a sigh.

{ISN'T THIS A TYPICAL LOVING MOTHER-SON RELATIONSHIP?}

50

Her life revolves around her daily talks with her two jailed sons (Yigal's brother Hagai, is serving a 12-year sentence for hollowing out the assassin's bullets, making them more lethal.) Attendance at the nursery school she runs from her home has dropped from 37 students to 17. Last year, on the anniversary of Rabin's death, someone torched the family car.

{COULD THAT SOMEONE HAVE POSSIBLY BEEN FROM THE SHABAK????}

Every other Monday, often accompanied by her husband, Shlomo, 56, a Religious scribe, she visits Hagai, 30, in a prison in Ashkelon, an hour and a half down the Mediterranean coast.

Every other Tuesday, she drives their '87 Suzuki for a five-hour round trip to visit Yigal, where she endures a thorough search by security guards. On the last visit, she said, a guard reached under her nutmeg-colored wig and extracted the pin that clasps her ponytail. It could be used as a weapon. *{YOU LET MY SON OUT OR I'LL PRICK YOU WITH THIS PIN.}*

On this particular evening, Hagai phoned home at 5:40, an hour before Yigal. Hagai sounded lively and engaged, compared to Yigal's humorless, apathetic tone:

"How are you, my soul?" Geula said, out of breath from bolting up 20 steps to the second-floor bedroom.

They began with small talk -- the underwear she brought him is too tight, He complained -- and moved on to politics. *{OF COURSE THEY DID. THAT'S THE PURPOSE OF THIS PROPAGANDA EXERCISE, ISN'T IT?}*

"What's new?" she asked. "There are rumors Yigal won't vote."

"I don't think I will, either."

{HAGAI TAKES A POLITICAL STAND. GEULA DOES NOT APPROVE. IT IS THE CIVIC DUTY OF HER SONS TO VOTE. LOOK WHAT THE STATE HAS GIVEN THEM.}

"During the last elections, Yigal said it was our moral duty to vote," said Geula. Both of the imprisoned Amir brothers voted for Likud candidate Netanyahu in May 1996. *{OF COURSE THEY DID. YOU CAN TELL BY ALL THE LIKUD POSTERS BOASTING OF THESE FINE SUPPORTERS.}*

"Back then we had hope, we had expectations. Do you expect anything from Netanyahu? I don't," said Hagai. "So let him lose. It'll be good. If Barak is elected, it will unify the religious right. No one will be able to stand up to them. Not one Barak, not a billion Baraks."

Geula told Hagai that she was going to speed up writing her book about the assassination. "Our economic situation is bad." *{OH NO. I'M GOING TO HAVE COMPETITION. I HOPE THE SAME HACK WHO WROTE THIS SCRIPT IS HER GHOSTWRITER.}*

"It's not bad."

"Not of the nation, you moron, the economy of our house." *{MORON? HOW LOVING! HOW NATURAL!}*

"You should describe the events of that period. People won't believe the crazy things that happened. It's like when you read a book about the British rule or the days of Stalin." *{GOOD ADVICE, SHAKESPEARE.}*

"Next week there'll be a holy rabbi in Herzliyya. I'll ask him what to do." *{UNDOUBTEDLY, A FINE LITERARY CRITIC AS WELL AS THEOLOGIAN.}*

"You can't tell anything from these prophecies," Hagai said.

"Last time I went to the rabbi for a blessing, he said, 'Don't worry, the boys will be freed soon.' He said he would live to attend your weddings."

"Yeah, well how old is he?" Hagai said sarcastically.

{START THE LAUGH TRACK. IT'S ABOUT TO GET BETTER.}

Before Hagai said goodbye to his mother, she reminded him that he would be allowed a rare visit with Yigal soon. "When we walk though to see Yigal," she told him, "they announce on the loudspeaker: 'Return all prisoners to their cells.' The area is emptied, not a soul allowed near us. Clinton! I always say the Clintons have arrived. We walk through -- whoosh -- like peacocks."

A Prison Authority spokeswoman said that the Amirs are isolated from the other prisoners because they fear one of the inmates might attack them. *{OR MAYBE YIGAL WILL OPEN HIS MOUTH AND SAY TOO MUCH.}* They have a private visiting room, down the hall from Yigal's cell, in a wing cut off from the rest of the prison. "When he murdered Rabin there was an outrage against him," said spokeswoman Orit Messer Harel. "The prison authority treats him fairly." *{THEY'D BETTER BECAUSE IF HE HAS AN ACCIDENT IN PRISON, NO ONE WILL BELIEVE IT.}*

He is allowed to receive mail, bundles of it, from teenage girls with crushes on the handsome assassin. They write to him, telling him their problems, and he writes back dispensing advice. One girl, his mother said, wanted to commit suicide. Another was upset because her parents divorced and her mother moved to France. *{HE SHOULD WRITE A DEAR YIGAL COLUMN.}*

Most of the day, though, Yigal just sits and studies Talmud, the books of ancient Jewish law. *{OF COURSE. AFTER ALL HE WAS A RELIGIOUS ASSASSIN.}*

"What are you going to do on election day?" Geula asked Yigal.

"What do I do every day?" he said.

"Study, study, study, study, study," she replied.

{YES, YOU SHOULD BE DOING SOMETHING CONSTRUCTIVE, LIKE THROWING A SOCK AGAINST THE WALL OR NON-STOP CALISTHENICS OR ANY OF THE OTHER OPTIONS AVAILABLE IN SOLITARY CONFINEMENT.}

He told her he had decided he is not going to vote: "It's a waste of time."

"The left will celebrate if Barak wins," said Geula, "and you'll be seen as a big failure." *{CLEARLY SHE SEES HER SON AS A BIG SUCCESS IN LIFE.}*

"So I failed," said Yigal, sullenly. "And everyone else wins."

"The right wins, too?" she asked.

"Ach, Mom, you take politics too personally," said the man who killed a prime minister. "It's all decided from above." *{NOW YOU FIGURE IT OUT??? AH, MOM?? YIGAL IS TRANSFORMED INTO BEAVER CLEAVER IN THIS FINELY CRAFTED SCRIPT.}*

"Yeah, but I'm living down here, below."

The other line rang. It was Amitai, Yigal's 12-year-old brother, calling from the central bus station, asking for a ride home: "Mom? Could you pick me up in Nof Yam?" *{AND HERE'S WALLY.}*

Yigal interrupted, offering from his maximum security cell: "You can take Bus number 29."

After the boy hung up, Geula told Yigal he had gone to the mall with his friends from school.

"The worst kind of friends," Yigal said. "What does he have to go to the mall for?" *{HE SHOULD HANG OUT IN RIGA, LATVIA. THAT'S WHERE THE GOOD KIDS ARE.}*

"Leave him alone. He hardly ever leaves the house. He's deathly afraid, Yigal, this period has been really hard on him. He is afraid to leave the house." *{GOSH, MOM. DOES THAT HAVE ANYTHING TO DO WITH ME?}*

"Bad friends," the assassin said. "Look after him. Don't let him just wander around with a bad crowd." *{HE SHOULD JOIN A SHABAK STRAW GROUP. IT'S FILLED WITH THE NEATEST GUYS AND LATER YOU GET TO BE A PATSY IN A POLITICAL ASSASSINATION.}*

The other telephone rang again. A girl named Elinor -- one of Yigal's pen pals -- was on the line. "Mom," Yigal said impatiently. "Connect her to me."

{GEE WHIZ, ELINOR. I TOLD YOU NOT TO PHONE ME AT HOME.}

Geula patched her son through. Then she put the receiver down on the couch and walked downstairs, leaving the two of them alone.

{WHAT, WITHOUT A CHAPERONE?????}

© Copyright 1999 The Washington Post Company

MY DAY IN COURT or
HOW I LEARNED TO DESPISE
THE ISRAELI JUDICIAL SYSTEM

Last October, Knesset Member Ophir Pines sent a letter to the Steimatzky Book chain, Israel's book monopoly, demanding that it remove my book *Who Murdered Yitzhak Rabin* from its shelves. In the letter he called me "the country's biggest inciter and his book is a pack of lies."

So I sued him for slander. A month ago he defended himself in court, citing parliamentary immunity. Or simply, no one can sue him for anything because he's a Knesset member. Judge Boaz Okun of the Tel Aviv Magistrate's Court turned down his defense and today, May 1, a procedural hearing was held. But wouldn't you know it, the judge had a change of heart and ruled that Pines was immune from further trial.

Here was my day. At 11 AM, my attorney Nitzana Darshan Leitner phoned from the court saying, "You won't believe it. The Attorney General sent his lawyer to influence the judge. He wants to speak to you. Can you get here in an hour?"

I did and she was right. Sitting at Pines' table were his two lawyers, but the General Attorney Elyakim Rubinstein had sent his mouthpiece, a curly-haired semi-youngish woman named Orit Podansky, to do 90% of the talking. She came armed with a brief prepared by the Attorney General's office explaining why Pines' parliamentary immunity had to be protected.

Nitzana received her copy of the brief three hours after the hearing began. "This," she acknowledged, "is called an ambush."

Later in the day, another attorney, Dror Bar Nahum, was incredulous. "I've never heard of the Attorney General intervening in a civil case before. This appears to be scandalous."

Before the afternoon session began, Nitzana informed me:

"He's already reached a decision. He wants you to comply with it so it won't be overturned later on. If you do, he'll waive court costs."

"What if not?" I asked.

"We'll appeal but it won't be cheap."

56

"Let's hear what he has to say first and maybe I can sway him to change his mind."

Judge Okun addressed me. "It would be a waste of time for you to carry on with your suit. It is legal in this country to criticize someone and anyone can legally write a bookstore asking it to remove a book from its shelves. There is no basis for a continuance."

I asked Nitzana, "Is it really legal?"

She whispered, "He's lying."

I asked for permission to speak and began, "Mr. Pines did not merely criticize me. He called me a liar and then deliberately abused his power as a Knesset member to wreck my income. I worked for almost four years on the book without pay and his goal was to deprive me of an income. To do so, he sent copies of his letter to Steimatzky to most of the Israeli media, and this resulted in headlines calling me a liar. There are hundreds of thousands of readers who still believe what's printed in the papers and they didn't buy my book because a member of the government said it was a lie. And, though I admit sales rose initially because of the scandal, later stores turned the book down because they thought selling it was illegal. I'll bring my publisher and he'll show you the refusals.

"Pines tried his best to ban my book. This is barbaric and primitive and has no place in the twentieth century. You seemed to have already made your ruling and it justifies book banning and the repression of free thought."

Judge Okun was clearly taken aback as was the gallery where loud murmurs arose. The judge tried a new strategy. Reading from the Attorney General's brief, he quoted my book's allegations against Carmi Gillon and Meir Shamgar. He had hoped I would trip up and say nasty things about them.

I replied, "So let them sue me. My fight in this courtroom is only with Pines. You can take passages you dislike and read them out of context but the fact is I based my book on police lab results, hospital findings and eye witness reports. I have brought my notes for you to examine. They prove I'm no liar since the book's quotes are from official sources."

The judge answered, "This isn't the time to read your notes. I haven't even read your book."

"It comes highly recommended," I said. Then I added, "Ophir Pines took an illegal action against me and even Leah Rabin called his act 'too drastic. People should read the book if they like.' Since the book's release, polls by Gallup and *The Jerusalem Post* show that two thirds of Israelis, including the Rabin family, want the assassination reinvestigated. If you rule against continuation of the trial, you will be alienating those with doubts. They will further lose faith in our judicial system."

Judge Okun replied, "We are dealing with technical matters here. This court is not the right place for you to pursue your argument with Mr. Pines."

"If a civil court isn't the right place, where is?" I asked.

"In the public arena," the judge replied.

I knew then that, yes, Judge Okun had been influenced by th government. He must have known how flimsy his arguments were Still, I added:

"And who in this public arena will compensate me for the damage Mr. Pines has done to my reputation and income? This court is the last stop. If you rule against continuation, you will set some very dangerous legal precedents. From now on Knesset members will be free to slander whoever they want and interfere in anyone's honest business affairs. That will be your legacy."

From that point on, Ophir Pines sat in the gallery with h assistant. The government sent in its forces and turned an hone judge into a compromised weakling. Attorney Avi Leitner summed up, "You just got a front seat view of judicial corruption."

For the next four hours, the lawyers entered their arguments but was already a done deal. Judge Okun ruled in favor of Pine parliamentary immunity and opened the door to dictatorship in Israe.

Now, of course, I'm ticked off so I'm going to release ne information. After unrelenting pressure from honest journalis Rabin's assassination night driver Menachem Damti agreed to interviewed by two television crews working with me, one from Tel Aviv University's Communications Faculty, the other from MGI Productions.

I had claimed that his daughter was in Rabin's car, slammed the back right passenger door, witnessed the murder and caused the Rabin limousine to arrive at the hospital between twelve and twenty minutes late. I based this assertion on an interview given to Channel Four Television in England on the evening of Rabin's funeral. One guest was Yifah Barak, who claimed her sister's friend was in the car, Rabin fell on her after he was shot, and she was taken to the hospital for treatment of shock.

Damti acknowledged that one of his daughters, Reut, was beside Rabin's car and indeed she appears in the assassination film standing beside her father. After all this time, Damti acknowledged that his daughter was at the murder scene but the film proved she wasn't in the car.

Next Reut Damti finally agreed to be interviewed and added to her father's claim that she couldn't have been in the car because she was outside. She was then shown Yifah Barak's interview and admitted that a lot of people did call her house on the murder night to see if everyone was all right. She added that there was nothing strange about her being in the sterile area, her two uncles were there too.

Damti had invited his family to witness the grand fake assassination of which he would play a starring role. One of his invited guests was likely his OTHER, twelve year old daughter.

Yifah Barak was phoned in London to get her side of things. She stood by her story but added vital details. She never claimed Reut Damti was in the car. Reut was her age. It was her sister Karen Barak who called the Damti home to inquire about the other daughter, who was her own age, twelve at the time. And that is who, most likely, was an accidental witness to the Rabin assassination.

Today was a sad day for Israeli justice but the push towards truth is now a shove. We'll all get there. And, oh yes...I SHALL APPEAL THE WRETCHED RULING.

GAGGING ON THE PROTOCOLS

So it looks like the Rabin truth is emerging. The symphony began with the Ophir Pines Overture in late October, in which the Knesset member abuses his powers to force the country's largest book chain to ban my book *Who Murdered Yitzhak Rabin*. This was followed by the melodious flurry of State Attorney General Elyakim Rubinstein's on-air banning of the broadcast of the protocols of a meeting his predecessor attended, during which he agreed to close a criminal file against the Shabak provocateur and likely Rabin murder conspirator Avishai Raviv. Finally came the glorious crescendo as the Rabin family—wife, daughter and son—all called for a reinvestigation of the Rabin assassination.

By the November 4th commemoration of the murder, the whole country of Israel was talking about the assassination more honestly than ever before. And while *Yediot Ahronot* printed banner headlines about the Rabins' demand for a new commission of inquiry, little old me was, as usual, deliberately snubbed. The most irritating snub was brought to me by the Channel Two morning show, which sent a crew to my home to interview me and then nixed my appearance.

However, Yuval Rabin saved the day. While being interviewed by the same Channel Two, he said, "Unless there is a reinvestigation there will be lots more Chamishes in the future." I was touched.

Now that the call is out nationwide for the air to be cleared, look who is getting on the new investigation bandwagon: Shimon Peres, Meir Shamgar and Eitan Haber. This is a good diversion strategy in the short term, or at least until they can contribute ideas on how to rig a new inquiry commission. Of this trio, the award for most unmitigated gall goes to Eitan Haber who wrote a piece in the November 7 *Jerusalem Post* about the "Still Unanswered Questions" surrounding the murder. This is what I wrote *The Post*'s editors:

Editors:

Surely Eitan Haber doth jest when he writes about "Still Unanswered Questions" surrounding the Rabin assassination? If not, the man has more gall than common sense.

Here is a summary of Haber's activities on the evening of November 4, 1995. After hearing of the shooting, Haber rushed to Ichilov Hospital, ran straight to the operating theater and collected

Rabin's blood-soaked belongings. At Rabin's funeral, the bloody song sheet was in Haber's hands instead of at the police forensics laboratory.

After absconding with the evidence at Ichilov, Haber rushed to the Prime Minister's office and emptied the file cabinets. When asked by *Kol Ha'ir* why he would do such a thing, Haber answered that he wanted to preserve Rabin's possessions for the IDF archives.

What a thoughtful act! Rabin wasn't dead ten minutes and Haber was thinking, "What can I put in the IDF archives for him?"

As a result of his actions and the sheer lack of any other explainable motive, many people accuse Haber of deliberate evidence destruction, a position I take in my book *Who Murdered Yitzhak Rabin*. Unless Haber can come up with a plausible explanation for his peculiar cleanup work on the assassination night, he would be wise not to comment on any aspect of the Rabin murder. He is included in the list of unanswered questions he has the nerve to write about.

(If you have any doubt about the veracity of my version of events, I will fax you documented proof, including Haber's own testimony to the Shamgar Commission. BC)

In all the excitement of the truth unexpectedly going public, the issue of the secret protocols has been too forgotten. It was leaked to MK Michael Eitan and he had intended to present them on Nissim Mishal's evening TV show. And he would have too if Elyakim Rubinstein hadn't slapped a gag order on the document in the middle of the show. Between banning my book and suppressing the public's right to information in front of a million members of that very same public, the government was clearly panicking or really, truly is bolshevist and undemocratic. Either way, these two actions alerted the public to the cover-up and set the stage for the Rabin family's bombshell two days later.

So what was in these protocols that is terrifying our political leaders? It turns out plenty and plenty more.

Allow me to present the gagged minutes of the meeting with my comments.

Summary of a Meeting
on the Swearing-In Ceremony of the Eyal Organization
Meeting Date: May 2, 1996

In attendance:

1. Attorney-General Michael Ben Yair
2. Noam Solberg - Senior Assistant to the Attorney-General
3. Edna Arbel - State Attorney
4. Talia Sasson - Head of the anti-incitement unit of the State Attorney's office.
5. N. Ben-Or - Head of the Criminal Division in the State Attorney's Office
6. Leora Chavilio, Senior Assistant in the Jerusalem District Attorney's office.
7. Chezi Kalo - direct GSS handler of Avishai Raviv
8. G. Ben Ami - GSS official
9. Eli Barak - Head of the Jewish Division of the GSS after Carmi Gillon, and during the Ya'acov Perry era, head of Perry's office.
10. Ledor, Jerusalem District Attorney

Just look who is seated around the conference table: Two of the slimiest characters in the Rabin drama, Eli Barak and Chezi Kalo, heads of the Shabak's Jewish Department, which not only ran Avishai Raviv and controlled Yigal Amir, but was responsible for a campaign of incrimination against "anti-peace" youths which resulted in crimes so heinous, they defeat the Rabin assassination in the category of immorality.

Not written is the fact that the meeting was in the office of the Rabin-era State Prosecutor Michael Ben Yair. Nonetheless, look who is in the discussions: today's State Prosecutor Edna Arbel. Recall, that this meeting was held just six months after the Rabin murder and keep in mind that the purpose of this meeting was ultimately to cover up that crime. What we have here is proof of direct collusion between the Peres government and two of the chief suspects in the Rabin assassination.

Synopsis of deliberations on evidence 133/95 The swearing-in
ceremony of the Eyal Organization, a document from 29.3.96 from
Leora Chavilio; the summary report of the Eyal swearing-in
ceremony; document from 5.2.96 from Y. Rodman

Attorney-General: We have all seen the videotape. Anyone who was
there, on location, could have understood that this was not an
authentic ceremony. Even the Shamgar Commission explicitly noted
this in its report.

Ben Yair makes it clear from the beginning that he knows a
televised swearing-in ceremony of the Shabak straw organization
Eyal, run by Raviv, was staged. Even Shamgar had to admit it. For
those unacquainted with the issue, a month and a half before the
Rabin murder, Raviv "inducted" new members of Eyal in a ceremony
where they swore to murder anyone who stood in their way of
sabotaging the so-called peace process. On the night of the murder,
Yigal Amir was identified as an Eyal activist and thus the public
accepted this as proof of Amir's motive to murder.

L. Chavilio: I didn't notice that the inauthentic sections were
intentionally edited out of the video. I see a problem with issuing an
indictment against the reporter.

Ben Yair's Jerusalem court representative, however, for some
reason, just can't see the phoniness of the tape and expresses doubt
about issuing an indictment against the reporter who filmed the
fraudulent clip, Eitan Oren.

A-G: Perhaps some disciplinary action can be taken against him?

C. Kalo: We are talking here about the handling of a problematic
agent. The loss-benefit evaluation looks like this: He served as our
agent for 8-9 years. Within this time period, he generally worked
well, except for the last year. He transmitted to us thousands of pieces
of information... During the last year, he lost control, and we were
able to nip the problem in the bud. He underwent an initial
investigation, and admitted [to his actions]. We continued to employ
him. As for the story of the videotape [of the staged Eyal swearing-in
ceremony] - from our perspective, this is a most serious episode. Our
officials deliberated on the matter, and decided that he was out of

control and that it was impossible to permit him to continue operating...

But we established new rules of operation... and that he would undergo psychological examinations. It was made quite clear to him that we wouldn't continue along the same path, and that he would not receive immunity for crimes he committed. In hindsight now, if we had gone ahead and broken off our ties with him, maybe he would have given us the murderer [of Yitzhak Rabin].

A court case against him would essentially be a case against the General Security Services (GSS). We would have to reveal all of our rules of operation, something that would cause serious operational damage. We have to remember that our opponents pose some serious threats today. During a trial, everything would come out into the open.

I don't remember any trial against a GSS agent that was conducted behind closed doors. Great damage could be caused—revelation of operational strategies, etc.

Jewish Department head Kalo makes a long, cliched appeal to quash any indictment of Raviv by citing various national security platitudes. What is of interest is how much Kalo lies to Ben Yair. According to his scenario, Raviv worked for 9 years with the Shabak and suddenly, just in the past year, he lost control and unilaterally initiated a long campaign of complicated and violent incriminatory scams. But his superiors didn't issue any of the orders. No way us!

Because Raviv was so naughty, Kalo and his fellow Shabak officers were going to fire him but darn, new regulations forced them to keep him on. In retrospect, it's too bad because if he had been released from duty, maybe he would have told us all about Yigal Amir's intentions towards Rabin. But, gosh darn, we kept him on and he just didn't want to inform us.

So you can't indict Raviv, even if he is guilty, because he's just a bad sort and we'll never hire his likes again. Promise. But if you put him on the stand, he could reveal all kinds of stuff that would endanger all the nice agents provocateur who infiltrate the Israeli Right.

N. Ben-Or: The attorney who represented Avishai Raviv will have a strong ideological bias, and it is possible that he would join forces with extremist elements, and that together, they would reveal secrets.

T. Sasson: They would do everything they could to reveal secrets.

G. Ben-Ami: As far as his criminal intentions are concerned: Did he intend to commit a crime? They suspected that Raviv was a GSS collaborator and he had to prove himself [to right-wing activists]. He had to remove all their suspicions that he was an agent. Dorit Beinish gave approval for his activities next to Bar-Ilan University, to incriminate someone else who would then be caught. He had to protect himself. Any Defense Attorney will call Raviv to the witness stand.

Now two State Attorney executives and a Shabak officer gang up to persuade Ben Yair to illegally suppress a dangerous criminal act because those Right wing meanies might actually expose "secrets," a code-word for other crimes. And worse, that could lead to charges against our good friend and playmate Dorit Beinish, the State Prosecutor, now a Supreme Court judge, who we learn, approved Raviv's earlier crimes. My, isn't the web of government collusion, not just in suppressing but in activating serious felonies, expanding? This could downright get out of hand.

E. Barak: Raviv was part of a violent group—the fact is that they suspected him of being a GSS collaborator. He had to, at all times, prove that he was as "active" as they were.

Yediot Ahronot did a deep expose of Eli Barak two weeks ago. He is a wife-swapper, stalker, drunk driver and liar. And he was just fired as Deputy Security Director of El Al for unspecified reasons, which possibly stem from El Al's fear that if the Rabin assassination truth breaks out, Barak would cause irreparable damage to the airline's image. He was given a high-ranking post in the Shabak and, we are warned, he is one of two officers being considered as next chief of organization. The same week that Barak got the boot from his job, the notorious Shabak chieftain and co-conspirator Carmi Gillon announced that he would be leaving his job as head of the National Insurance Institute to take up duties as director of the Shimon Peres Center for Peace. The announcement was celebrated by a three page article in *Ha'aretz* painting Gillon as a cross between Mother Theresa and Santa Claus.

> Ledor: We have to close the file "due to lack of public interest." An indictment [against Raviv] could seriously harm the GSS. We have to accept the GSS opinion on this. We close a lot of files in this manner, due to a "lack of public interest." The harm is clear—the trial would look crooked. Holding it "behind closed doors" just won't help.

We now learn that the Attorney General's Office closes lots and lots of criminal files with the all-purpose excuse that the public wouldn't be interested in the facts. It's a much cleaner foil than rigging a trial that the public would know was "crooked." And these are the heads of the Israeli judicial system talking.

> Ben-Or: I am bothered by the criminal aspect of this—I am not sure that it won't end in a finding of "not guilty." Then we will be in a strange situation. This person was working in a problematic situation. His involvement in Eyal was illegal. They didn't allow him to bring television cameras. A police agent who is commissioned to 'buy' drugs is not allowed to smoke them himself, etc. When you're in the trenches, though, it's difficult, and sometimes [an agent] will "give himself permission" to break a law. Maybe he will argue the defense of "necessity," maybe the justification that he had to "earn the trust of those around him." I don't want to make a decision about his criminal culpability.

> A-G: We see this as a serious matter. I don't dismiss the damage to the organization [the GSS]. Even the revelation of his code name caused great damage. But the additional damage is relatively insignificant, and we can make an effort to minimize it. It is possible to conduct proceedings behind closed doors. The case itself is very serious and there is a real public interest in filing criminal charges. This episode shocked television viewers and caused enormous damage, a virtual public storm! I just don't see how we can avoid beginning [criminal] proceedings.

Remember, Ben Yair admits there IS public interest in Raviv's case. He is the only one at this meeting trying to talk truth.

> Ben Ami: Another factor [that must be considered]: The GSS ability to hire agents, and the organization's handling of already existing agents. Our sources demand that the Service ensure that they will not

be revealed. It will be hard [if Raviv goes to trial] to handle present agents and hire new ones.

A-G: Sec.(b)(1); The whole trial will take place behind closed doors. The Shamgar Commission was also held behind closed doors. It is possible.

Ben Yair finds a compromise. Raviv will be tried behind closed doors. Nothing involving sensitive security issues will be released. But even this isn't good enough for the forces ganging up against him.

Sasson: Let's assume that there is evidence. The television clip made an impression on me. We see from Chezi Kalo's words what kind of damage [such a trial] would cause to the GSS. I must work with the assumption that there would be such damage. We have to weigh the benefits [of bringing him to trial] against the losses. It has to be evaluated in cold [objective] terms.

E. Arbel: From the perspective of the Attorney-General and the State Attorney's office: It is impossible to evaluate the evidence when we know that what is available there does not give an accurate portrait of what went on. The man was an agent. We don't know what the true picture was at the time. We can't know the clear details of the situation until he gets up on the witness stand, and maybe he will say that he was operating according to the directions of the GSS. It is impossible to say whether there is or is not evidence against him. The file [swearing-in] was staged. The lines were not clearly demarcated for Avishai Raviv. What would have happened if he would have prevented the murder? With all the difficulties that this [decision] entails, I am not sure that we can accomplish our goal. With a heavy heart, I suggest we close the file [against him].

And here we go. Israel's current State Prosecutor, the one with the heavy heart, Edna Arbel, votes for cover-up. And what worries her? Raviv could tell the truth and testify that he was just following the orders of his Shabak superiors...who were just following the directions of the Prime Ministers, Rabin and Peres. It is for them that Arbel asks what difference it would have made if we could have saved Rabin or not. The important thing is "accomplishing our goal" and Ben Yair apparently knows what she means.

A-G: Section 4(a) - I don't see a problem with the evidence. I don't see any problems in terms of his criminal intent. It is impossible to close the case without public exposure.

Ledor: Some time ago, we put together a format that we could use for a situation in which we announce that a file is being closed.

Arbel: It is simpler to defend the closing of a file due to a lack of evidence; it is possible that he [Raviv] wanted to convince them that he was "one of them." I see a problem with this. And if there is a problem with the evidence, it is easier to explain things [to the public]. I don't have to wait and come to the Court for it to say all this. My desire is to issue an indictment, but the risk is so big. We can in fact explain this to the Supreme Court; it's possible to defend [such an approach].

E. Barak: In actual fact, during the entire time that Raviv served as an agent for us, there were many "incidents." He could very well testify about the [numerous] cases in which we gave him directions. The entire story of his service will be revealed, and there will be legal difficulties. Even after the [Eyal] television broadcast, they continued to employ him.

Barak admits that Raviv knows too much to be fired. If he opens his mouth, the real Rabin assassination could spill out of it. Or the real Kahalani brothers' case or the real story of Baruch Goldstein's setup to take the blame for the Hebron massacre, etc., etc.

Sasson: A "lack of evidence" and a "lack of public interest" together constitute good reasons [for closing the file]

A-G: I don't want to be involved in closing the file. I won't get into explaining. In any case, we have to send a letter to the Israel Broadcast Authority in which we express our bad feelings at the video clip [the swearing in ceremony of Eyal]. We have to write something against [TV reporter] Eitan Oren. I can't be involved in this. Were I to be the only one to decide, I would issue an indictment. But, as I said, I don't want to be involved in this. I would like to request that the issue be transferred over to the State Attorney's office, that the State Attorney's office make a decision on this, and issue a statement to the plaintiffs.

So Ben Yair weasels out of responsibility for closing Raviv's file. He lets Beinish do that. And she does eventually for lack of public interest, the very pretext Ben Yair previously admits is not true. If he had his way, boy things would be different. But heck, he's only the Attorney-General, the man responsible for supervising justice in Israel. What does he know about law anyway?

LEAH RABIN CONFESSES

Look at paragraph two of this *New York Times* article by Leah Rabin:

Two Leaders Must Reshape Their People's Dreams
By Leah Rabin
(Reprinted from *The New York Times*, July 18, 2000)

The history of the Middle East is marked by bloody wars and breakthroughs for peace. But breakthroughs do not occur by chance. Rather, leaders who recognize the futility of war, leaders who have peered into the faces of victims who will not return, are prerequisites for peace. Intimate knowledge of the pain of war must also be coupled by the courage to conduct a process that will not always be accepted by everyone, or more accurately, will engender formidable controversy. Menachem Begin and Anwar Sadat were such leaders. And so was my husband. Yitzhak Rabin, may his memory be blessed.

No one will forget the day on the White House lawn, sun blazing, when Yitzhak Rabin and Yasir Arafat shook hands, a symbolic act that set the peace train on its track. The handshake was wrenching for both leaders, but it broke down the barriers of mistrust and fear. Brokered by President Clinton, the Oslo agreements infused the spirits of the people with hope and established a new reality of dialogue built on cooperation and mutual respect. The three lethal bullets *{!!!}* that killed my husband were intended to kill not merely the life of one man, but to deter other leaders from traversing the road to peace.

Mrs. Rabin confesses that her husband was shot three times. Now let's do the math. According to the Shamgar Commission findings and most witnesses, Yigal Amir shot three times. According to the same Shamgar Commission findings and from the alleged victim himself, the second shot hit Rabin's bodyguard Yoram Rubin. So Leah Rabin is reporting an extra shot, a shot the Israeli government denies ever took place.

Of course, my central proof that Rabin was not shot by Amir is that Rabin was shot three times and Amir never shot him three times. So, thank you Leah for verifying my research. She now joins Shimon Peres, who as I previously reported, testified on a PBS documentary which I hold, that Rabin was shot three times and once from the front, another act Amir could not have done. It seems everyone who should know the facts, is agreeing with me lately.

Why did Leah Rabin tell the truth to *The New York Times* when it so clearly exonerates Amir? The best guess is that she is preparing the public for the day when the third shot becomes an open issue. The strategy is to defuse the third shot evidence by pre-convincing the readers that Amir shot all three bullets into her husband. She needs reminding that he didn't according to the government's commission of inquiry because he couldn't have. Most likely, she already knows that.

Still, save this quote. Now Leah Rabin is trapped by her own words.

The Reluctant Investigator

Last week I met a former advisor to the Israel Police Criminal Laboratory, who told me he had used his police connections to gather powerful new evidence of the conspiracy to murder Rabin. I was joined at his apartment by Natan Gefen, author of *Fatal Sting* and by a nationally known TV reporter and his researcher. The advisor was more than telling the truth; he possesses some of the most stunning evidence I have seen in many months.

I brought some of my latest finds, including Peres' self-incriminating PBS interview and the Channel Four Britain interview with Yifah Barak, which places Rabin's driver's 12 year old daughter in his car as a witness to his murder. The advisor asked to record my tapes and I agreed instantly. My policy is not to hold onto any evidence but to distribute it as quickly and widely as possible.

However, after he showed us some examples of what he possesses, he refused to give me copies, explaining that he was planning to sell them one day to some, as yet unfound, television network. I told him that for my first two years, I took a heavy financial loss concentrating on my Rabin investigation and only since last January had book sales and lectures finally begun supporting my continuing research. I added that my first motive was saving our nation from control by murderers, and that all the leading researchers shared my philosophy and freely exchanged information as it came in.

The next day, I spoke to him and told him outright that I found his attitude unappealing and would not continue with any working relationship that was so one-sided. He explained that he had to pay his bills but would give me the evidence I had seen on condition that I promise not to publicize it. I didn't agree. Our nation is on the verge of withdrawing to undefendable borders and dividing its capital. There isn't time for ego or profit. The Rabin murder truth is the only weapon I see that can bring down the regime of evil, and if this researcher had his own personal agenda, then I would not cooperate with it.

That said, I can only report what I saw, but I'm certain Natan Gefen will be only too happy to act as a witness for my veracity.

The advisor showed us a set of pictures from the so-called sterile area where Amir shot his blanks, just minutes before the staged assassination took place. These photos were presented to the Shamgar Commission but were banned from publication. The three outstanding pictures were:

*   Leah Rabin is photographed descending the steps with her husband. Officially, she was separated from him at the top of the stairs. This is now proven untrue. I am uncertain of the significance of this fact, but it indicates that Mrs. Rabin is not telling the whole truth about her husband's murder.

*   Far, far more exciting, Menachem Damti's 12 year old daughter is captured on film. A few months ago, Damti told a TV crew that his 17 year old daughter at the time, Reut was in the sterile area but refused to confirm or deny that his other daughter was also there. In the Kempler film, we see Reut Damti standing beside her father and she is taller than him. The girl in this photograph is considerably shorter and younger than Reut was. YES, it's proven!!!! Damti's other daughter, the accidental witness to Rabin's murder in his car, WAS IN THE STERILE ZONE!

As the evidence catches up with him, Damti is cracking. A source close to him has informed me that he has become unstable and his behavior is threatening his job and marriage. Further, his teenage daughter went missing recently and was found by the police. She was returned to Damti with the warning that he "had better watch her carefully."

*   About two minutes before Amir's shots, Shimon Peres is photographed in deep conversation with Yuval Schwartz, the mystery

man of the assassination. This is Agent Yod, who Shamgar ordered suspended from his job with the Shabak. He was head of security for the rally and took much of the heat for Rabin's murder. And, as I have been recently informed by someone who was there, he was YIGAL AMIR'S COMMANDER IN A GOLANI COURSE!!!

And there they are together in the photo; Schwartz, tall, husky with curly black hair and a very concerned looking Shimon Peres. Now we ask why Peres would have anything to say to the head of rally security at that moment. All Peres had to do was get in his limousine and go home. Why was he showing such great concern about rally security when the event was already over? That Peres had personal ties with Schwartz was revealed in a throwaway sentence from Carmi Gillon's lying book, as I have previously noted. As I stared at the photo of Peres and Schwartz in deep conversation, I saw that those ties had led to something far more sinister than Schwartz ever planned.

If the advisor chooses to put his nation first, I will distribute these photos. Until then, three other people saw them and will agree that my descriptions are accurate.

I'll close on a suspicious incident. This morning I visited my accountant. On the way to his office I noticed a sign on a door reading "Movement for Quality Government". I had heard this organization was fighting government corruption, so when my appointment with my accountant was over, I dropped in to see if they would join the fight to expose the Rabin murder truth. Here is the conversation I had with the director:

"I won't talk to you about the Rabin assassination. I saw what I saw and know who did it."

I replied, "I have documentation from the hospital and police that what you saw isn't what happened. Have you read my book?"

"Yes, no, I've read about it and I won't go near it. The only people I'll pursue are the rabbis who incited Amir to murder Rabin."

"Rabbis?" I asked. "Are you aware of Avishai Raviv? He was a tiny cog in the incitements generated by the Shabak."

"I don't want to hear that nonsense. The rabbis murdered Rabin."

I don't know what this organization is a front for, but it's certainly not connected in any way to seeking quality government.

CHAPTER 6

WAITING FOR RAVIV TO SING

THE AVISHAI RAVIV FILE

Though on July 6, Avishai Raviv will stand trial for the misdemeanor of "not preventing a crime," in fact he incited violent crimes and there are numerous witnesses to his methods. The following crimes can be proven beyond doubt if the Israeli judicial system truly seeks justice:

*   Avishai Raviv, a Shabak agent since 1987, committed perjury at the trial of Hagai Amir, by testifying that he had never been employed by the Shabak.

*   Avishai Raviv organized two phony television reports, directed by Eitan Oren and approved by IBA GM Moti Kirschenbaum, purporting to show a swearing-in ceremony and summer camp of the notorious radical right-wing group Eyal. For both the false reports and for establishing Eyal under false pretenses, Raviv is incredibly guilty of fraud. If the state prosecutor wants to pursue these crimes, he/she simply has to call former Eyal members to the stand to testify to Raviv's methods.

*   Avishai Raviv distributed a poster of Yitzhak Rabin wearing an SS uniform at a large political rally on October 5, 1995. He gave the poster to Channel One reporter Nitzan Khen, who would make a fine state's witness, if the prosecution pursues justice.

*   Avishai Raviv hounded Yitzhak and Leah Rabin, holding Friday afternoon vigils outside their apartment and threatening to hang them in a public square like the Mussolinis.

*   Avishai Raviv and Yigal Amir organized numerous "learning seminars" together, the largest one, in Hebron, drawing 600 participants. At these gatherings, Raviv was heard by hundreds of witnesses both calling for Rabin's murder and prodding Amir to do it. Among the witnesses the prosecution could call are the students of

Sarah Eliash's girls seminary, who have already testified to the Shamgar Commission about Raviv's vocal threats to Rabin's life and his provoking of Amir to commit the murder.

* Avishai Raviv testified at the Shamgar Commission that he did not tell his superior officers about Amir's intentions towards Rabin. The officers thus claimed that they were ignorant of the facts. Yet others did inform on Amir, including a soldier in the Intelligence Brigade and a fellow Eyal activist. Despite Raviv's testimony, it is impossible that the Shabak was ignorant of Amir's activities. An honest prosecutor would call Shlomi Halevy to testify that he reported Amir's intentions directly to the Shabak on July 6, 1995, and hence neutralize Raviv's anticipated perjured testimony to the effect that he kept his officers in the dark about Amir's declarations.

* Avishai Raviv's activities were approved by the Ministry of Police, which ordered 15 complaints against him closed and by the Justice Ministry which refused to allow Yigal Amir's lawyers to subpoena him as a defense witness at his trial. The cover-up of his crimes runs deep in the Israeli political system and this is the prime reason why his trial will likely be a travesty.

Possible Deeper Crimes:

Three years ago, a television report showed a close-up of a 9 mm Baretta held by Amir in a photo and the serial number matched that of the gun used by Yigal Amir to shoot blanks at Rabin. Witnesses place Raviv with Amir behind the stage at the fatal Tel Aviv rally some twenty minutes before Rabin descended the steps. It is thought by many that Raviv handed Amir the gun filled with blanks. Rumors also have Raviv entering the Machpela Cave with Baruch Goldstein in late February 1994.

These issues and others are beyond the scope of Raviv's July 6 trial but are worthy of deeper police investigation. The preceding list of Raviv's proven crimes are relevant, even to the flimsy charges for which he will stand trial. If they are not addressed by the prosecution, the Israeli judicial system will stand accused of deep misjustice.

LET'S TWIST THE NEWS AGAIN, LIKE WE DID LAST SUMMER

TEL AVIV, Israel, April 25 (UPI) — The Israeli Justice Ministry has filed charges against a former security agent, Avishai Raviv, accusing him of failing to inform his handlers an extreme right wing activist intended to kill then-Prime Minister Yitzhak Rabin.

The real charge should have been incitement to murder. Raviv's crime is perfect for the state. If he didn't inform his handlers, well, then he's going to take the rap for the real murderers, his handlers and those who gave them the order to knock off Rabin. Of course, we all know he really did tell his handlers because he was not merely a security agent but a Shabak officer. As for Amir being an extreme right wing activist...no, he was an intelligence asset working hand in hand with Raviv to incriminate those pesky settlers and other opponents of the Oslo Accords. All in all, UPI got nothing right in its opening paragraph.

Rabin, a Nobel Peace laureate, *{WHO CARES?}* was shot in 1995, disrupting the peace process. *{THE PEACE PROCESS WAS DRAMATICALLY REVIVED AFTER THE MURDER, IF THAT IS WHAT IS MEANT BY DISRUPTING IT, WHICH IT WASN'T}*. His *{CONVICTED/ALLEGED}* killer, Yigal Amir, is serving a life sentence.

The prosecution charged Raviv, code named "Champagne," after years of hesitancy. The General Security Service feared that even a trial behind closed doors would expose its ways of handling agents and collecting intelligence, and hamper chances of recruiting more agents.

So that's the only reason Raviv wasn't indicted after three years? If the trial was conducted behind closed doors, who would be privy to the "ways?" Certainly not the public or potential Shabak recruits. Maybe there were other reasons for the "hesitancy" like exposing everyone who knew of Raviv's activities and approved them, i.e., Dorit Beinish, Michael Ben Yair, Yossi Sarid, Benny Begin, Moshe Shahal, and Rabin himself, just for starters, or a whole who's who of the Israeli ruling establishment.

77

However, allegations that the GSS itself was involved in a conspiracy and provocation to murder Rabin made its head, Ami Ayalon, change his mind.

The proper phrase is public pressure. Ayalon changed his mind because of the unrelenting evidence released proving that the GSS itself was involved and polls showing that a third of the public believed this was the case. With all the political, judicial and media power assembled to cover up the truth, the evidence was winning. So a phony trial with Raviv testifying that he was the only one who knew about Amir's intentions was viewed as the better option than continuing with the crumbling cover-up.

The charge sheet filed with the Jerusalem Magistrate Court says Raviv had been a member of the now-outlawed extreme right wing Kach movement. The GSS recruited him in December 1987 to foil violent activity.

More violent activity had been committed on behalf of the conventional political parties. It was Raviv's duty to infiltrate Kach and turn legitimate political protest into extralegal political extremism.

Raviv, who studied at Bar Ilan University near Tel Aviv, befriended Amir, who studied law there.

Not according to Amir. In his testimony to Shamgar Committee investigators, Amir claimed that no one was taking Raviv seriously until HE took over Eyal's organization of political seminars.

The charge sheet says that in their discussions on "the effective way to prevent the implementation of the Oslo accords" with the Palestinians, Amir repeatedly said Rabin ought to be assassinated. Following several murderous attacks on Israeli civilians, Amir said he would kill Rabin.

Wrong. The Witnesses at the Shamgar Commission who attended the Raviv/Amir seminars testified that it was RAVIV who repeatedly announced that Rabin ought to be assassinated. Amir assented occasionally in a begrudging manner. Of course, far be it from UPI to actually read the protocols of the Shamgar Commission.

The charge sheet alleges that Raviv told his handlers of Amir's role in anti-government demonstrations, but did not report the murder threats.

That is because Amir's Shabak handlers Carmi Gillon, Chezi Kalo and Eli Barak coordinated their testimonies and perjured themselves at the Shamgar Commission. Each testified that Raviv told them nothing of Amir's murder threats. Raviv backed them up by testifying that he didn't take Amir's threats seriously. For this crime, failing to recognize a serious murder threat, Margalit Har Shefi was sentenced to nine months in prison. Raviv could get the same and be well rewarded after for taking the blame...unless the prosecution actually gives a damn and subpoenas all the witnesses who saw Raviv in action, and then the bluff will fall to pieces, In such a case Raviv will have to explain why he was energetically inciting young people to murder Rabin. If so, the state will be hard-pressed to explain why Raviv was standing trial for merely failing to prevent a murder. Ideally the judge will sentence him to far more than nine months unless he spills the beans. But this is Israel so don't hold your breath. Adir Zik has written in *Hatsofe* that such a contingency has been considered and witnesses have been terrifyingly threatened not to open their mouths at the trial.

> Raviv is also accused of encouraging a terrorist organization by establishing an extreme right wing group, Eyal, that "encouraged violence that could lead to a person's death."

The person's death that he could have led to was not Rabin's. Rabin is skipped over and Raviv is now accused of encouraging acts that could have led to the death of an Arab. See the next two paragraphs.

> A declassified report by a State Commission of Inquiry about Raviv's activities, published in November 1997, says his handlers knew he had also harassed and assaulted West Bank Arabs, but little was done to restrain him.

> The 1997 report said Raviv was known for "puncturing Arabs' tires, assaults...overturning stalls, beatings with brass knuckles....He took an active part in that activity and said many Arabs were severely hit by him."

Raviv was not tried for most, but not all, those attacks because his handlers reckoned he provided important information on extreme right wing Jewish activities. They persuaded the State Attorney not to press charges against him, the report said.

There you have it; one pathetic indictment. In order to surveil Jewish radicals, Raviv went a little too far in his role of being one himself. Naughty, naughty. And he should have reported Amir's threats to Rabin's life but he was much to busy making them himself to pay attention.

HOW THEY ARE PLAYING WITH US:
ISRAELI JUSTICE IN ACTION

I just called the Jerusalem courthouse and guess what????
Surprise, surprise!!!! Avishai Raviv's September 1 trial has been
delayed until October 3. How fortuitous for those hiding the truth.
Raviv was supposed to be tried on July 6 but so many people planned
to sit in the courtroom as witnesses that the date was changed until
September 1. The excuse given then was that the prosecution was
denied sensitive evidence that he discovered was vital two days before
the trial. This time the court spokeswoman didn't even bother with
any flimsy pretext. Fear not, on October 3 the many witnesses who
had planned to scrutinize the trial on July 6 and September 1 will be
sitting in court.

Let's not call it a coincidence that the delay was granted one day
after the Supreme Court not only turned down the Amir brothers'
appeal for a review of their sentences but actually increased their
combined prison time by seven years. Now how would you like to
have Yigal Amir's lawyer Shmuel Fleischman working for you?
Here's what he told reporters about his client: "I have not heard him
express regret. He believes that what he did was the right thing." Now
that's a lawyer determined to defend his client with all his skills!

So let's compare what the same Fleischman told NBC-*Extra* in
1997: "This is Dallas and JFK all over again. I believe in twenty or
twenty five years there will be a brand new point of view about the
assassination."

My, what a change of heart in two years.

Last Friday I lectured before an audience of media people
organized by Channel Two producer Ilana Ziv. One well known
reporter from *Ma'ariv* told me after, "You seem like a nice guy and
you may be right. But I'll never read your book because what you're
doing is wrong."

Such journalistic ethics! They are almost as moral as Israeli
judicial ethics.

RAVIV DEFENSE IS THE TRUTH

Since the Avishai Raviv trial is being held behind closed doors, or putting it in more accurate terms, since the Israeli public is being denied the right to know what is going on at Raviv's trial, I will do my best to follow the proceedings via the flimsy summations released to the public weekly.

After the first two hearings, which began on February 22, it is clear that the prosecutor Moshe Shiloh is running the government's cover-up. Raviv's lawyer Eyal Shomroni-Cohen complained bitterly that the state prosecutor is not releasing most of the documents requested for Raviv's defense.

No surprise so far...but look at what Shomroni-Cohen is requesting!!!! I quote from the weekly newspaper *Makor Rishon*:

> Attorney for Shabak agent Avishai Raviv, Eyal Shomroni-Cohen has demanded a copy of the State Pathologist's Report on the death of Yitzhak Rabin. He also demanded copies of the other medical reports. He announced, "Until I see these reports, until I examine the actual murder, I won't sleep at night and will disbelieve the murder." The prosecutor has charged Raviv with not preventing Rabin's murder and Shomroni-Cohen observed that his client cannot defend himself unless the murder itself is examined. Although he has not claimed there was a conspiracy, Shomroni-Cohen stressed that, "A major question is raised within the documents." He added that the documents he is demanding challenge the accepted version of the Rabin murder. He pointed out that Rabin's daughter, the Knesset member Dahlia Rabin-Pelosoff stated that there is a clear contradiction between the State Pathologist's Report and those of Ichilov hospital. He accused the state prosecutor of denying him the documents based on the protection of personal privacy. He noted that the right to defend oneself in a court of law takes precedence over personal privacy.

Well, well, well, well, well. Look who has discovered the Rabin assassination conspiracy thesis! And give Raviv's attorney credit for defending his client properly. If given access to the very same documents I have published in the Hebrew and Russian versions of my book *Who Murdered Yitzhak Rabin*, Shomroni-Cohen will prove his client is innocent of not preventing Rabin's murder because Amir didn't commit the murder. If he wants copies of said documents, all he has to do is call me. We wish him good luck and some of us are going to press and press and press for this trial to be opened to the public and media. Please do your part.

My good people, based on my recent experiences, the Jewish people are waking up and are demanding to know the truth. In the past two weeks I gave three lectures in the NY/NJ area to packed houses. Hineni House in Manhattan was filled to its back corridor, while 250 inquiring souls heard me at the Bnei Yeshurun Synagogue in Teaneck. I got on a plane home and a day later 250 people arrived for my lecture in Gush Katif. Since then, I have given my speech non-stop to audiences up and down the length and breadth of Israel and the invitations to speak keep pouring in. The court may be hiding the Raviv trial, the media may be covering it up, but the people want to know the truth already.

Raviv's trial may be hidden but the issue of how Rabin really died will not go away until the facts are known. I leave you with two brief items recently relayed to me:

1. Charles Bronfman is paying millions to send American Jewish college students to Israel for free under a program called Operation Birthright. He is selling the plan as a charitable gift to the Jewish people but many of the first 6000 who arrived in Israel are reporting that they were subjected to a sophisticated propaganda exercise designed to instill a love of the Israeli left and the unpopular "peace" process. Students complained that their requests to visit Judea and Samaria were turned down. One tour guide told me that the vast majority of the guides hired by Bronfman were from the far left and touted the "Peace Now" line to their trapped students. Bronfman's brother Edgar is a leading member of the Council on Foreign Relations. He and two other CFR members, Lawrence Tisch and Henry Kissinger provided the initial funding for Ehud Barak's political career in 1995.

2. While it is known that Yitzhak Rabin's deal with Hizbullah after Operation Accountability included the right to kill IDF soldiers, it was widely reported that shelling Israeli towns or dropping Katyushas on them was forbidden by the pact. That is not precisely the case. Hizbullah agreed not to bomb almost all towns including Metulla, Nahariya, Rosh Hanikra, kibbutzim such as Dan and Daphne, etc., which support the Labor Party and whose residents are mostly

Ashkenazi. However when Katyushas had to be launched, they were restricted to the mostly Moroccan, right wing city of Kiryat Shmoneh. Hizbullah has stuck to the deal and only Kiryat Shmoneh has borne the brunt of the rockets for nearly the past decade.

AVISHAI RAVIV HAD A TRIAL - SORT OF

The best news about Avishai Raviv's October 3 hearing was the crowd that came out to witness it. They filled the chamber and forced security personnel to leave an impressive cluster of people in the corridor. And that crowd clearly surprised those employed to try and judge Raviv. The prosecutor, Moshe Shiloh, constantly complained that he was restrained from explaining his case by the unexpected outsiders and he even suggested the court be cleared. Those who sat in the chamber were insuring that justice be done.

Before the hearing began, the majority of the pundits expected a done deal. Raviv would confess to the two charges against him: not preventing the murder of Yitzhak Rabin and creating an inciteful organization, Eyal (Jewish Warriors). He would admit that he didn't know of Amir's murderous intentions towards Rabin, thus did not inform his superiors in the Shabak (General Security Services). As a reward for his honesty and regret, he would do some cushy public service work and the Shabak would be saved.

There were a few optimists who were certain a trial would take place immediately. This hearing had been postponed twice since July, plenty of time for both sides to have their cases fully prepared. These hopeful few spoke of being in court until at least next week.

Raviv entered the courtroom without a kippah on his closely cut hair, so all pretense of him being actually religious were dropped. After the camera crews, all two of them, backed off and left some space, I stared closely at Raviv's face. Then he stared back at me. I supposed that he was well aware of my book on the Rabin assassination, since it concentrated so much on his crimes and must have played a role in his sitting in the court at that moment. He outstared me; I had to avert my eyes. Despite the fact that his provocations on behalf of "peace" led to a depth of suffering seldom, if ever, felt in a country that has felt more than its deserved share of pain, he was one scared, confused young man. His eyes and expressionless face told of countless hours of threats to his being if he sang at this trial, years of cynical manipulation and subtle to overt mind control. He had to be wondering how he got into this mess, if he had enough cerebral independence left to wonder.

Included in the crowd were other people who had helped bring Raviv to trial. They included Adir Zik, the *Hatsofe* and Arutz Sheva journalist who had relentlessly pursued him for four years, reporting his every move publicly. He even set up a Raviv hotline, allowing callers to report where they had last seen the thug. Seated next to me was media watchdog Yisrael Medad, who had taken an important aspect of the Raviv affair, a staged, televised Eyal swearing-in-till-death initiation ceremony, to the Supreme Court. In the row behind us was Arieh Zaritzky, an executive of the Professors For A Safe Israel, who had awakened the academic community to the real Rabin murder facts and thus given a "conspiracy theory" legitimacy among academia.

Now, since members of this court audience had no doubt that Raviv was a monster, we were quietly rooting for the prosecutor Moshe Shiloh. Some thirty years older than the defense lawyer, Eyal Shomroni-Cohen, he benefited from the respect that comes with age, a friendly visage and occasionally, a humorous wit.

As for Shomroni-Cohen, well, we knew he was a Shabak mouthpiece who appeared at the home of Yigal Amir's parents on the very night of the assassination, took $2000 from them to defend his son, absconded with it and ended up being Avishai Raviv's lawyer. On top of that he was young, humorless and rather smarmy looking. And of course, we had no doubt his client was guilty, and that didn't help his image problems.

So we looked for sinister motives when he complained that the prosecution was blocking him from meeting with former GSS chiefs Ya'acov Perry and Carmi Gillon, and that he was denied access to 1300 pages of printed material, including unreleased portions of the Shamgar Commission findings. He insisted that Perry and Gillon were central to his case since in the past, and in order to escape trials of their own, both had claimed that Raviv was totally unaware of Amir's plans for Rabin. And he doubly insisted that he had a legal right to peruse the prosecution docket to plan his own argument.

Before Shiloh stood up to reply, I did think to myself, why wouldn't he want Perry and Gillon on the stand? Isn't this what the trial is supposed to be about? Doesn't he relish the opportunity to tear the Shabak honchos to bits to get to the bottom of what Raviv's real crimes entailed? Then I had a thought. If he did that, eventually he might get to the real truth—that Rabin's assassination was initially supposed to be staged, that Amir shot blank bullets and that someone took advantage of this "exercise" to murder Rabin in actuality.

The thought passed almost unnoticed as Shiloh listed the usual national security excuses for not releasing witnesses and testimonies to the defense. Then Shiloh made an offer; he would allow the defense full access if it agreed not to publicize the material and only in the presence of a security officer from the Shabak or Justice Ministry. As for the Shamgar Commission findings, he had no authority to release them to the defense.

At this point Judge Amnon Cohen, who led the panel of three justices, turned down the offer of a Shabak or Justice Ministry security officer, stating that he would appoint an appropriate security observer from the court. So, we asked, what makes him so distrustful of, not so much the Shabak, which was expected, but of his ultimate employer, the Justice Ministry?

Shomroni-Cohen also became agitated that Shiloh did not name which rabbis he was going to call as witnesses. When asked why, he replied that Amir's intentions towards Rabin were well known throughout the religious community, and without giving away his line of defense, Raviv was being picked on because he was a Shabak agent.

At this point Judge Cohen observed:

"Shabak agent or not, it is a crime not to report the impending murder of the Prime Minister...Now I want to know, did your client know about Yigal Amir's plans to shoot the prime minister, yes or no?"

For the first and only time in the session, there was a restrained gasp from the audience when Shomroni-Cohen replied, "No."

Raviv was planning to defend himself. There was no deal. He didn't confess. A trial would take place.

Then we fell back to earth. Shomroni-Cohen requested the right to appeal to the Supreme Court to release the secret sections of the Shamgar Report before the trial began. Judge Cohen sighed, smirked and said:

"I barely have control of this court, let alone the Supreme Court. But two months should be enough time for them to answer your petition. The trial will begin, then, in December."

Though not necessarily. If the Supreme Court waited longer, the trial could begin as late as February. We left the courtroom in great agitation, almost all of us convinced that we had seen another delaying tactic by Raviv's lawyer and the judges. But Professor Zaritzky sorted things out to my satisfaction.

> "That's not what happened," he insisted. "It was Shiloh who was trying to cover everything up. His strategy was to deny Raviv access to the most sensitive witnesses and documents and rush a judgement through. The only way the truth will come out is if Raviv is in a fair fight. The judges ruled for the defense every time and they were right. From now on I'm watching out for the prosecution and cheering for Raviv to press a strong defense."

An epiphany: RAVIV IS INNOCENT OF THE MAIN CHARGE AGAINST HIM. He did not know Amir was going to murder Rabin and, in fact Amir did not murder Rabin. Raviv knew only of a FAKE murder attempt. If he pursues the truth to the end, he will be acquitted. If they let him.

I had bowed to Zaritzky's superior analytical skills. And I had to bow twice. Right afterwards, a demonstrator outside the court building, Itamar Ben Gvir came up to me. He had to be angry. In my book I quoted sections from three sources: The Shamgar investigation report, the court protocols of Yigal Amir's trial and police records; all of which record Amir testifying that on the night of Rabin's murder he was informed that Avishai Raviv gave right wing activist Itamar Ben Gvir a gun loaded with blanks and he intended to shoot it at Rabin.

> "Do you know the trouble you caused me?" Ben Gvir asked. "My parents read the book and they were deeply distressed. I was beaten up at a rally because people thought I was a Shabak agent. I never knew Amir. He tried to tie me in to the assassination because I knew Raviv too well. It was all disinformation. Don't you see that I'm just another victim of Raviv and that's why I'm here today?"

At that moment, I did see. But I didn't stop doubting.

CHAPTER 7

ANOTHER FRENCH CONNECTION

CARMI GILLON'S ATTEMPTED ESCAPE

The cover-up of the Rabin assassination reached new and even uglier heights of deceit in yesterday's (April 14) Israeli newspaper media. Both *Yediot Ahronot* and *Ha'aretz* published long interviews in their weekend magazines with former General Security Services (Shabak) legal affairs director Shabtai Ziv. My, what a coincidence, two papers, same obscure character. And just a few days before *Yediot Ahronot*, as was emblazoned on its front page headline, would publish two chapters of former Shabak chief Carmi Gillon's new book on the Rabin assassination in its Passover magazine.

You can just feel the terror in Shabak headquarters as the fumbling high officers mapped out a full media blitz to quash the widespread and accurate perception that Gillon was one of the conspirators behind Rabin's murder. In fact, Ziv admits that the current Shabak chief Ami Ayalon did not try to prevent the trial of Yigal Amir's partner in provocation and crime Avishai Raviv because "He was tired of hearing about the conspiracy theory."

What is so useful in these media cover-ups, are the facts that don't get cleaned out of the final copy. Ziv told *Ha'aretz*, as he did *Yediot Ahronot*:

> "I can state that all the activities of a judicial character in connection with Raviv were done in consultation and full transparency vis-a-vis the state attorney and her department. A number of discussions were held about him in which we gave the Justice Ministry all the information we possessed about offences he committed..."

This isn't new, I made the same claims in my book *Who Murdered Yitzhak Rabin*. But then, I wasn't the head of the Shabak's legal affairs department. Ziv's remarkable admission means former Justice Minister David Libai and former State Attorney General Dorit Beinish and her staff were apprised of Raviv's crimes and provocations and approved their continuation. This justifies indictments against them all as active accessories in innumerable crimes. Yet how does one issue indictments against the people who issue indictments?

And Ziv, as was clearly requested by his authorities, went out of his way to compliment Carmi Gillon: "He is a humane and sympathetic gentleman," he insisted.

Well no, actually he's a bit off here. Gillon is a brutish and cruel gorilla. He is also an inveterate liar, which is why I am presenting a truer picture of him than his own book will. Gillon will claim that the Rabin assassination was a series of blunders and he felt so bad about it, he offered to resign the next day. He will paint a picture of a murderous anti-peace community that had to be infiltrated by the likes of Raviv to protect Israel's glorious democracy. He may even claim, as he once did, that he never even met Avishai Raviv. So before anyone has a chance to believe this liar, permit me to paint a truer picture of the monster.

How He Became Shabak Chief

In 1990 Gillon wrote an MA thesis at Haifa University on the dangers the Israeli Right present to the nation. More than a few people have insisted the thesis was written for him, just as his post assassination newspaper analyses on peace clearly were. At the time, he was head of the Shabak's Jewish Department and he was utilizing Avishai Raviv to infiltrate various borderline groups such as Kach and the Temple Mount Faithful.

However, someone very powerful had bigger plans for him and after the Hebron massacre of February 1994, Gillon became Shabak chief. Of course, in a fair world that would have been impossible since, as Jewish Department head, he had supposedly failed miserably to prevent the massacre. In fact, he had succeeded but this is not the place to explain how Dr. Baruch Goldstein was set up to take the blame for bloodshed planned by others.

The one sticking point was Rabin, who opposed Gillon's appointment vehemently. So Gillon had Avishai Raviv organize a protest against his home in Mevasseret Tzion to place him in contention and Rabin agreed to his appointment only if then-Shabak head Ya'acov Perry supervised his tenure, an unheard of procedure. Rabin admitted that Gillon's lack of experience dealing with Arab terrorism made him unfit for the post but he gave in "because of cabinet pressure." Which in the cabinet of the day meant that Shimon

Peres supported Gillon. Today Gillon is the chairman of the Shimon Peres Institute for Peace. All in all, while head of the Shabak, Gillon was a Peres plant.

Now let us look at Gillon's activities and his central role in the Rabin murder according to Israeli experts. We begin with Adir Zik writing in *Hatsofe*:

"Carmi Gillon was the direct handler of Avishai Raviv for an extended period. It was he who turned Raviv into the biggest provocateur in Israel's history...

"Even while Gillon's deputies directed Raviv, Gillon was in direct contact with him. He ordered him to marry a Russian-born settler as a cover for his activities.

"Gillon ordered Raviv to undertake a long series of violent crimes against Jews and Arabs in Hebron, Jerusalem, and at Tel Aviv and Bar Ilan Universities.

"Gillon ordered Raviv to make violent attacks on Knesset Members Tamar Guzonsky and Shulamit Aloni on behalf of the Shabak front organization, Eyal.

"Gillon's hatred of the Right led him to utilize the services of a Shabak plant in the Israel Broadcasting Authority named Eitan Oren, to film and televise a series of phony reports whose goal was to humiliate the residents of Judea and Samaria...

"Gillon ordered Raviv to print a photomontage of Rabin in a Gestapo uniform and display it a huge anti-government rally. Rabin called Gillon to his office and demanded an explanation. Gillon told Rabin not to worry, Raviv was under his authority.

"Immediately after Rabin's murder, Raviv told police investigators that he had heard Amir threaten Rabin's life four or five times. Raviv had to have informed his superiors, including Gillon about Amir's intentions and they had to have deliberately ignored the warnings."

Gillon's Uncanny Predictions

On August 24, 1995, barely two months before Rabin's murder, Gillon told a group of journalists that Rabin's life was in danger from an assassin. He described this theoretical murderer: "He doesn't have to be a settler, he could be a dark-skinned Sephardic student, studying at Bar Ilan University and living in Herzliya."

What powers of precognition hath the prophet Gillon! Why Amir also was a Sephardic Bar Ilan student who lived in Herzliya! Ophir Shalakh of *Ma'ariv* was but one of many of the attending journalists who noted, "The profile Carmi Gillon presented precisely described Yigal Amir."

And who can forget Gillon's classic reaction when informed of the murder by phone while he was in Paris (*Yediot Ahronot*, September 24, 1996): "It was a Jew." However did he know?

What Was Gillon Doing in Paris on the Assassination Night?????

Gillon's Shabak underlings were widely quoted claiming to have queried Gillon why he was flying to Paris two days before the most security-sensitive rally in the country's history. He refused to answer but did order his deputies not to change even one detail of his procedures for the rally.

Gillon has consistently refused to explain what he was doing in Paris but a correspondent of mine found one revealing quote, the only one of its kind. Gillon explained that he was visiting Ya'acov Perry in a hospital in Paris. Very touching. But if true, it means both the current Shabak head and his predecessor were in Paris the night of the assassination.

I have traced the tracks of the Rabin assassination to Paris. The goal of the murder was to place the French puppet Shimon Peres in power. And Gillon was there pitching in. He was later rewarded for his connivance and silence, when in 1999, Peres appointed Gillon at a huge salary to chair his peace institute.

Trying the Wrong Man

Mati Golan wrote in *Globes* (December 11, 1997):

"Carmi Gillon is opposing the indictment of Avishai Raviv because it would reveal Shabak operating procedure. Perhaps he is right, Raviv shouldn't be on trial, his superiors should be."

However, the State Attorney General did finally indict Raviv on two minor charges in 1999. When he announced the indictment, he added a strange addendum: "We found no justification for indicting his superior, Carmi Gillon."

Fear not my friends, I will be reviewing Gillon's book chapters after they are published. Barring a most unlikely confession, we'll sort Gillon's lies out. After that, I will have a chance to prove which version of Rabin's murder is right, his or mine, in a court of law.

Last October MK Ophir Pines publicly called my book "a pack of lies" and used his influence to have it banned, albeit, most temporarily. So I sued him for slander and three weeks ago, my attorneys Nitzana Darshan and Avi Leitner won a major legal victory. Pines contended that as a Knesset Member, he was immune from prosecution. The judge turned down his argument.

On May 1, 8:30 AM at Tel Aviv District Court, the judge will rule if I can continue my suit. If he does so rule, I will prove that I'm no liar by calling every character in the Rabin assassination to the stand, including Gillon. Recall when reading Gillon's chapters that he would never take that kind of risk. Watch this: Carmi Gillon, I am calling you a liar and a conspirator in a political assassination. PLEASE SUE ME... See, nothing happened.

CARMI GILLON'S PATHETIC LAST STAND

I had dreaded reading Carmi Gillon's book about the Rabin assassination because of the anger it would generate within me. Instead, after reading it, I just felt pity for the head of the Shabak (General Security Services) at the time of the murder. That's because his lying version of the events is so pathetic. Even the extreme left-wing *Ha'aretz* newspaper condemned the book in its weekend paper, in two separate columns, for being self-serving and insincere.

Of course, *Ha'aretz* is incapable of reporting what actually befell Rabin so the criticism was typically shallow. Nonetheless, it's becoming clear that nobody likes this book. Poor Carmi. Here are a few of the lies that illustrate his desperate need to free himself of the widely perceived burden that he was a conspirator in the murder.

* Gillon writes that he only met Avishai Raviv, Yigal Amir's partner in provocation and the highest ranking Shabak infiltrator in the anti-Oslo camp, once. Gillon served as head of the Jewish Department which ran Raviv for five years but he only ran into his most valued informer one time and that was accidentally. And that's the best he can offer to save his worthless skin.

* Gillon insists that he ordered the surveillance and repression of left and right wing radical groups equally. He adds that he personally preferred the right wingers because at least their motives were patriotic. In all the years that Gillon ran the Jewish Department and then the whole Shabak, I can't think of one left wing activist who was arrested. But I can think of a lot of right wingers, all innocent of crimes, who were incarcerated without charge. Shall we begin with the 17 members of the phony Jewish underground, all later released as innocents, the Kahalani brothers, recently released from prison for alleged good behavior, Shmuel Cytryn, who served four months in solitary confinement for publicly exposing Raviv as a Shabak officer, etc., etc. Gillon's attempt at equanimity is, well, pathetic again.

* Gillon claims he advised PM Peres to open a public inquiry into the Rabin murder. Not according to every other source I've read. He tried to head off such an inquiry with a self-cleansing internal investigation and only public pressure forced Peres to reject this ploy and initiate his rigged Shamgar Commission of Inquiry.

*   When informed of the murder, Gillon was told, "And you won't believe it, he's from Herzliya." Gillon explains that he had previously told numerous people that "the assassin could come from Herzliya or Dimona." Nice try Carmi but it won't fly. In late August 1995, Gillon informed a gathering of reporters that Rabin's life was in danger and the potential assassin could be, "a dark skinned Sephardic student of Bar Ilan University who lives in Herzliya." Every point true to the patsy Yigal Amir. A statistician informed me that according to his computations, the odds of Gillon getting all the information right without knowing that Amir was being set up to take the rap were some 24 million to one.

*   The Italian journalist Aldo Baquis called me and emphasized just how badly Gillon handled the issue of Shlomi Halevy. He was a soldier from the Intelligence Brigade who, in early July 1995, was informed of Amir's vocal threats against Rabin and reported them to the Shabak. Aldo pointed out that on page 256, Gillon claims that it was a shame the Shabak didn't take Halevy seriously. Just three pages later, he does an about-turn, writing that the Shabak did take Halevy very seriously and were on the lookout for a curly-haired Yemenite at the rally.

Now here is where Gillon gets good and tripped up on his lies. He claims that based on Halevy's meager description, it was impossible to identify Amir because "there are lots of curly-haired Yemenites." What he forgets to mention but Halevy didn't, is that he told the Shabak Amir was a member of the radical organization Eyal. If they had wanted to, the Shabak could have arrested Amir that day. What Halevy didn't know was that Eyal was a straw group created by the Shabak, led by the Shabak officer Avishai Raviv, and its social director was the Shabak asset Yigal Amir. But Gillon sure as heck knew all that and it's not in the book. All that appears is one more pathetic falsehood.

My friend, the journalist and author Joel Bainerman, phoned with another observation: even the insignificant points in the book look made up. Gillon begins his flawed attempt at a masterpiece of deceit with the following story:

Four days before the assassination Rabin sent Gillon to Paris to meet with French Intelligence. They were worried about Algerian terrorists and needed the advice of an Israeli expert. Rabin felt good relations with the French were vital and ordered Gillon to go, despite the security concerns about the upcoming Tel Aviv rally.

Joel points out that Rabin despised the French and made no secret of his feelings. He felt that they were conniving with Peres to overthrow him. But as Joel astutely noted, at least Gillon backed my claim of the past four and a half years that Gillon was in Paris meeting with French Intelligence. However, I more than suspect that the meetings had nothing to do with Algeria and a lot to do with overthrowing Rabin.

Gillon's chronology of the assassination night runs like this: At 10:00 PM, Israel time, while he was on the way to the airport, the chief of personal security Benny Lahav phoned him to tell him Rabin was shot. He got on the plane stunned. He had planned to arrive in Israel in the wee hours of the morning and inspect El Al security but cancelled the plan. Instead, he was left all alone in his thoughts. The El Al stewardesses knew who he was and did not disturb him during the whole flight.

These are the delusions of a cornered rat. Nothing rings true. According to his arrest record, Amir was in custody at 9:30. Shamgar puts the time at 9:40. So the head of the Shabak had to wait between twenty minutes to half an hour to be informed of the shooting. And shucks, that ruined his plan to get off a five hour flight and inspect El Al security at 3 AM. Officially, all of a few dozen people outside the Shabak knew Gillon's identity and position. Publishing these facts was a criminal offence. Yet all the El Al hostesses were all in on the secret and were so concerned they broke international airline regulations and didn't disturb Gillon for five hours, not even when drinks and dinner were served.

And that's how desperate this pitiful creep is!

Here's Gillon's strategy. He blames the government for not taking the recommendations of the first Shamgar cover-up, the Commission of Inquiry into the Hebron Massacre, seriously. He blames Rabin for not listening to him and wearing a bullet-proof vest. But most of all, he blames his underling Shabak officers and the bodyguards under their command for being so ill-prepared to stop the murder.

The guilty Shabak officers in Gillon's version of the true conspiracy are Head of Personnel, Dror Yitzhaki (and by the way, he is not alone in his suspicions; they are shared by some investigating the truth about the murder), the Head of Personal Security, Benny

Lahav; Head of Operations, Adi Azoulai and Commander of Rabin's Security, Yuval Schwartz.

The only person who comes out squeaky clean is Shimon Peres, whom Gillon falsely claims was almost a victim of murder at the rally as well. Gillon recommended the suspension of these four officers and Peres agreed, and this is telling, "though he was closely associated with all of them."

That is Gillon's way out and in all likelihood, he is immune from retaliation because everyone he attacks is hiding his own assassination secrets. The strategy he employs is actually clever. Though he seemingly attacks Shamgar for not going far enough in his inquiry, all his facts about the murder are directly quoted from the Shamgar Commission. An example; he repeats over and over again Shamgar's false finding that Rabin was shot from half a meter's distance. The Israel Police Criminal Laboratory proved beyond doubt that Rabin was shot point blank. But since Amir never, ever shot from point blank range, he does not include the truth.

One reading of this miserable exercise is Gillon is hinting that his trip to Paris was arranged to get him out of the way so his underlings could get on with their hanky panky. Another, more likely reading, is the Shabak fell apart when he wasn't there.

And that is the true sophistication of the book. By blaming Shamgar and Rabin's bodyguards, he is reinforcing the lie that the assassination was all a big snafu. He should be made to know, it won't work. One day, he will himself, be investigated for his real role in Rabin's murder.

PERES: THE LEGACY LINGERS ON

RIGGING THE '96 ELECTIONS

How complacent we acted after Peres was defeated in the presidential vote. One victory and people think the "peace" process is over. So, let's face reality. Peres will be back, and a terrified Barak must obey his Council on Foreign Relations masters and push through their war plan at any cost. As he told CNN, "If the Israeli people turn down our referendum, we'll find another way."

On the plus side, our strategy is having an effect, even if the mainstream media refuses to acknowledge it. Yesterday, I was at the butcher shop when the personal aide of a religious Knesset member walked in. With a huge smile he said, "You don't know the balagan you caused."

A month before the presidential vote, the unsung heroes of the Goldberg Family of Tel Aviv and Tsfat faxed my article "Peres Must Never Become Israel's President" (see page 108) to all 120 Knesset members. Within I listed Peres' crimes, ending with his organization of the Rabin murder with the operational cooperation of the French intelligence services. I was reliably informed that the faxes helped turn the vote.

Now we close in on the kill. We prove Peres' role in the murder and there is a way. So far, I have documented Peres' ties to the main assassination conspirators: Shabak chief Carmi Gillon, who Peres appointed to chair his peace center; Yoram Rubin, Rabin's bodyguard and shooter, who Peres appointed to head his bodyguard unit on the assassination eve, no doubt because of the fine job he did protecting Rabin; Peres' personal chauffeur Menachem Damti, who took Rabin on his last drive; and Jean Frydman, who paid for Rabin's final rally and helped organize its security.

This is very heady circumstantial evidence but there exists solid proof of Peres' hand in the murder...and it cost him the 1996 elections.

The Rigger Gets Rigged

In the March 14, 1994 edition of *The National Review* is a three-page article by Joel Bainerman and me called "The Peres Gambit". In it, we prove that Peres rigged the 1992 elections and here's how we found out.

A number of months earlier, Yehoshua Meiri, a journalist for the left wing newspaper *Chadashot*, had an article printed within called "Beilin's Secret Journeys". Meiri claimed that in June 1990, Yossi Beilin, then Shimon Peres' deputy, flew to Cairo to deliver a letter from Peres to Arafat. Peres offered the PLO a state if it would use its influence to shift Israeli Arab votes to the Labor Party or its allies in the next national elections. After three more Beilin trips to Cairo and the personal intervention of Secretary of State James Baker, Arafat agreed. The Arab parties won only four seats, compared to ten today, the rest of the Arab vote went to Labor and the Zionist far left. The PLO provided the difference in the vote which put Labor in power and the Oslo process was put in motion.

Joel and I met Meiri several times and he provided solid documentation, including powerful tapes he secretly recorded. *The National Review* checked our sources and we passed their scrutiny. Several months later, reporter Steve Rodan followed our lead and interviewed Meiri at length. Like us, he found Meiri entirely credible and his evidence airtight. The result was a series of scoops in *The Jerusalem Post* that verified Joel's and my findings. Peres had indeed rigged the 1992 elections and the PLO was allowed to determine the future of the Jewish State.

But in 1996, the tables were turned on Peres. Natan Gefen in his book *Fatal Sting* recounts how he took the smoking gun Rabin murder document, the surgeon's report proving Rabin was not shot twice in the back as our government insisted, but three times and once frontally, to Likud MKs Ehud Olmert and Dov Shilansky. Neither was interested and Shilansky told him, "We don't need the report, we've already fixed things up." Gefen concluded that the Likud had the proof and had already blackmailed Peres into throwing the upcoming elections.

Independently, I received confirmation of this seemingly fantastic claim. In April 1997, our internal security force, the Shabak organized a violent protest outside a speech I was to give about the Rabin murder at the Hebrew University of Jerusalem. A few days later, I received a call from Ya'acov Mor, a self-admitted Shabak graduate who told me, "If the guys were willing to do that to you, you must be on to something serious. I'd like to see what you've got."

Mor was the financial advisor for the Minister of Social Affairs, Eli Suissa. He came to my home and I gave him a stack of documents to peruse. After a half hour, he put his index finger on his mouth and with his other hand directed me outside. When we left my property he said, "I'm not talking in your house. Do you know your documents are authentic?"

I replied that I did.

"And do you know how high up this must go?"

I answered that I had an idea.

"Why don't you have a job in Nepal or Uganda? That's what they usually do to troublemakers? I'll report my findings to my minister and we'll see what he decides."

A few days later, Suissa's secretary called. She invited me to the minister's office and asked that I bring my documents for them to photocopy. In return, I would receive the most sensitive information of the whole Rabin affair.

How could I refuse? I was driven to Suissa's bureau, handed over my documents and was seated in his chief aide's office. I heard an energetic discussion in the corridor and then the young aide, Yitzhak Sudri, today the Shas Party spokesman, entered with Mor. He said:

"The minister cannot attend this meeting but he has authorized me to inform you that the following information is accurate."

This was Sudri's exposition. In February 1996, four months before the elections, disgruntled Shabak officers passed the documents I had acquired plus many more to the "top" of the Likud leadership, which must have included Netanyahu and Sharon. They organized a meeting with the "tzameret" or top of Labor's leadership, which must have included Peres and his campaign managers Ehud Barak and Haim Ramon. After presenting the proofs, the Likud proceeded to blackmail Labor over Peres' role in the Rabin assassination.

If the name Rabin was used in Labor's campaign, the Likud chiefs would release certain damning documents to the public. If Peres defeated Netanyahu in their television debate, other documents would be released. And if Peres won the elections, everything would be released.

Labor did not bring Rabin's memory into the contest, Peres gave a miserable performance in the television debate and Netanyahu won the elections though he really didn't.

Recall the election night. The declared winner, Peres, did not show up at the Tel Aviv Cinemateque to thank his supporters. However, the declared loser Netanyahu, all smiles, addressed his followers with the prophetic words "Don't worry. There's plenty of time until the morning when the government will change."

And he was right. That day someone leaked the results of one polling station to Meretz MK Ran Cohen. He discovered 1500 spoiled Labor votes and many forged Likud votes. Based on this one station, he estimated that at least 120,000 were stolen from Labor. He submitted a petition to the Supreme Court to recount the votes but his own party ordered him to withdraw it. Even Peres prevented a recount though he publicly was dismayed that "Labor supervisors weren't properly represented in the polling stations."

Sudri gave me the name and phone number of a graduate student at Tel Aviv University's Faculty of Law, who was writing his thesis on this scam based, in part, on the Likud's own reports of their blackmail of Peres. We met in a deserted cafe and he informed me:

"I was warned yesterday not to supply you with any documentation. The best I can do for now is confirm that the elections were tainted. Peres actually won by 2%, just like the polls predicted."

A month ago, at my lecture in Bet Shemesh, an election supervisor stood and, before 90 people, confirmed the election rigging. "A colleague of mine told me he was ordered to destroy piles of Peres votes in 1996." And that is why in three and a half years, the Netanyahu government did not pursue the Rabin truth. They were now soiled by blackmail and election tampering.

The only reason Peres and Labor would have taken the dive is if the blackmail against Peres worked. And it only could have worked if he had knocked off Rabin.

An investigation into the 1996 elections would require interrogating Suissa, Mor and Sudry. Let them deny the meeting with me took place. Who knows, perhaps they will do the honorable thing and not perjure themselves. I also have the names of the law student and election supervisor. I'll supply those as well. It is the ideal way to nail Peres for good. All that's missing is a responsible body willing to investigate these charges.

THE CONFESSIONS OF JEAN FRYDMAN

There may be a dozen people in Israel with the power and influence to have organized the Rabin assassination. Of these, only Shimon Peres has direct ties to the main actors of the murder. Consider the most likely of the plotters:

* Carmi Gillon - Head of the Shabak (Security Services) at the time of the assassination. Despite being forced out of office for incompetence by the Shamgar Commission of Inquiry, Peres appointed him chairman of his peace center.

* Yoram Rubin - Triggerman of the murder. Despite being head of Rabin's personal bodyguards, those who failed to protect him, on the very night of Rabin's murder Peres appointed him to be head of his bodyguard unit.

* Menachem Damti - Rabin's last chauffeur, whose trip to Ichilov Hospital took twenty times longer than it should have. In fact, Rabin cancelled his regular driver Yeheskiel Sharabi 90 minutes before the fatal rally and he was replaced by Damti, who was the regular driver of Shimon Peres.

* Jean Frydman - Peres' French financier, who funneled millions of dollars into the Ifshar Fund to promote the Oslo process. His partner in Ifshar was Tel Aviv mayor Shlomo Lahat, strangely, a Likud Party member.

In my book *Who Murdered Yitzhak Rabin*, I examined the roles of Gillon, Rubin and Damti in close detail. I only touched on Frydman when I quoted his bizarre statement; "I have such guilt feelings, I can't sleep." After acquiring a copy of an interview with Frydman from the *Paris Match* (16/11/95), we can all understand why.

I will quote from Frydman's own words and comment after:

> I am a member of the real peace camp. I have been so for the past four years at the urging of my good friend Shimon Peres, a man I like very much. We agreed that Israel's military occupation was negating Jewish values and demoralizing our youth. Shimon, a peace now man, was with me on the joyous day in Tel Aviv that the Norwegian

Foreign Minister, Jorgen Holst, revealed the protocols of the agreement signed with Arafat. Peres didn't believe the agreement would hold and felt it could be derailed. I remember him telling me, "It's now up to Israeli public opinion. We need to quickly form an organization that will sway the Israeli people." I replied, "It's all yours."

The Norwegian Foreign Minister Jorgen Holst was the first murder of the Oslo Accords. In excellent physical shape, he died at 53 of an unexpected heart attack. A widespread rumor said he died of knowing too much. Frydman, a media tycoon, out of the goodness of his heart, gives Peres a carte blanche for his plan to brainwash the Israeli people in the summer of 1993.

Peres immediately flew to California to convince Secretary of State Warren Christopher of the reality of the Oslo Accord. Both he and Clinton were skeptical of the agreement reached behind their backs. Once they realized Peres wasn't bluffing, Clinton said, "Now your problem is Israeli public opinion."

For some reason Peres had to fly to California to get Christopher and Clinton's permission to mount his and Frydman's propaganda campaign. In short, he told the two Council on Foreign Relations reps, "The French have agreed to fund the campaign. We need your approval and mass marketing experts." The rest of the paragraph is nonsense. I interviewed one of the Oslo negotiators, Ron Pundak, and he told me he phoned Christopher from the very first evening of the talks in January 1993. The State Department guided the negotiations from their inception.

After the Taba Accord, I realized that Israeli public opinion was in the hands of the far Right. Then at a rally of the right wing Likud, someone displayed a photomontage with Rabin in an SS uniform. Others shouted, "Death to the traitor Rabin."

When told of the incidents, Rabin was furious. He was well past fear but felt an injustice had been done to him.

On Saturday, October 6, I was at Shimon Peres' home. I told him, "We cannot leave the streets in the hands of the Likud and far Right. We have to put up a fight."

Since the Taba Accord, which gave Egypt a hundred extra yards of sand in the Sinai, became law, it is hard to see how public opinion was in the hands of the far Right. After that, the lies come thick and heavy. The photomontage and death threats came from Shabak provocateur Avishai Raviv and the minions of his straw group, Eyal. Rabin knew this and was not furious at the far Right but at Carmi Gillon for his illegal use of Raviv. According to research by Israeli journalist Adir Zik, Rabin ordered Gillon to his office and let loose a barrage of invective against Gillon, to which Gillon assured him that Raviv and Eyal were under tight control and were his responsibility.

So Frydman's account of Rabin's reaction is a flagrant falsehood. Because the State Prosecutor has mounted a cover-up of Eyal's crimes, we cannot be absolutely certain that Peres was apprised of them. However, it's a pretty safe bet that Peres knew everything Rabin did plus much more about the Shabak's covert war on the settlers. After all, he and Frydman were organizing the public relations side of things. So, in all likelihood, every word of Frydman's is a conscious lie.

On Monday, Shimon and I were in Rabin's office. He asked me one question: "Will you take responsibility for this great event?" I told him, "Yes, on condition that I do it the way you want." Rabin and Peres gave me the green light. "Let's go," they said.

With Lahat, we organized a dozen generals for our Israeli Woodstock, our war for peace.

I suggested to Rabin November 4th as the date of the event, but he hesitated. He had an official dinner. Finally, he reorganized his agenda and accepted. I wish I had not arranged things for the day of his death.

If Rabin already had a commitment, who was Frydman to insist he change his schedule? Frydman does not explain why he was so insistent.

We distributed posters reading "Say Yes To Peace, Say No To Violence, Kings of Israel Square, Tel Aviv." We constructed a large stage, and a grand podium. We worked with the security personnel assigning 750 police officers, 250 border guards, sixty elite sharpshooters and three helicopters to patrol the skies. This was in

106

addition to the Shabak forces that permanently protected Rabin and Peres. We placed special detection equipment at each entrance of the perimeter.

Frydman and Peres organized the security of the rally. If there were 750 police officers, all but a few were directed away from the sterile area where Rabin was shot. If there were metal detectors at the entrances, they were not placed backstage. If the crowd was well lit, some people arranged for the sterile area to be bathed in darkness. And Frydman confesses that he was one of those people. And why not? He paid for the rally.·

Peres' close ties to the murder now extend past the head of the Shabak, the driver, and Rabin's bodyguard right to the very person who organized the security for the assassination rally. And from there, to France.

WHATEVER IT TAKES,
PERES MUST NEVER BE ISRAEL'S PRESIDENT

In the Fall of 1989, a Geneva-based French arms dealer named Eduard Seroussi paid Ezer Weizman over $3 million to fly to Geneva and meet the PLO, thus initiating the disastrous "peace" process with the most notorious terrorist group on the planet. Although accepting a bribe is illegal in Israel, Weizman was not charged with selling his country out. Rather, the Attorney General recommended this week that he resign. So, Israel was spared the spectacle of its President tried and then shackled off to prison. The leading candidate to replace Weizman is Shimon Peres and if he is finally chosen, this time Israel will not be spared the spectacle. Peres will be tried and watch out, because this time around it will be for murder.

Israel's moral imperative will be shattered in the wake of the trial. It will suffer a national collapse of conscience. Peres cannot become President!!!

Please utilize the following brief resume to fight the looming disaster.

* Throughout his career, Peres has enjoyed the company of gangsters. Whenever he traveled to Paris, he would be wined by the likes of such wanted criminals as Marc Rich, Pinchas Greene, Bernard Cornfeld and Bruce Rappaport. It is the latter who should have ended Peres' career for good.

In 1985, Iraq could not export its oil because Iran had blockaded the Persian Gulf. So it turned to Bechtel Corporation to build a $30 billion pipeline to the Jordanian port of Aqaba. Bechtel would not initiate the project unless it had assurances that its investment would not be destroyed by Israel in warfare.

Enter Bruce Rappaport, who the FBI charged with oil sanctions busting. He made his fortune selling oil to the West from countries whose oil was officially forbidden from sale. Hearing of Bechtel's quandary, he acted as a middleman between then-Prime Minister Peres and US Attorney General Edwin Meese. Peres bribed Bechtel, offering a written promise never to bomb the pipeline in exchange for $700 million, to be deposited in the coffers of the Israeli Labor Party.

When word of the bribe leaked, Meese was forced to resign his government post, but Peres, as usual, escaped untarnished.

* In 1986, a government commission headed by Abba Eban investigated the Jonathan Pollard spy affair. Eban placed most of the blame for the scandal on Peres who knew of Pollard's role, read his intelligence as it came in, used it to build international policy and, as Prime Minister, ultimately authorized the operation. Peres spent a week denouncing Eban, rejected the commission report and threw Eban out of the Labor Party, thus ending his political career.

* During the same period of Peres' 1984-86 term as Prime Minister, he authorized Israel's participation in what became known as Iran Contra. Israel's role included selling arms to Iran and funneling the money to Central America, where the likes of Michael Harrari and Yair Klein had acquired controlling roles in the cocaine trade. Iranian cash bought cocaine sent by the tons to the US, much through a little used airport at Mena, Arkansas, under the watchful eye of Governor Bill Clinton. The coke money was laundered and used to buy weapons for the Nicaraguan Contras...hence Iran-Contra.

Peres sent his terrorism advisor Amiram Nir to Teheran where he was joined by the likes of Col. Oliver North and Bud MacFarlane, whose goal was to convince the ruling mullahs to release American prisoners held by Hizbullah in Lebanon in return for arms vital to the war effort against Iraq, procured from Israel's stocks. Ultimately the deal collapsed though Israel did forward two shipments of Hawk missiles to Iran.

The scam became a national scandal in the US and Nir was subpoenaed to testify before a Senate Commission investigating Iran-gate. The Israeli government did its best to prevent its participants from flying to Washington but Nir was determined to set matters straight. In anger, Peres locked Nir's office and released him from public service.

Days before Nir was to fly to Washington to testify before the investigating committee, he died in a small plane crash in Mexico. Of the three passengers, he was the only one to perish. A writer with an Israeli intelligence background, Arieh Ben Menashe, claimed in his book that Peres ordered the murder.

* In Yitzhak Rabin's 1979 book, he called Peres "an unrelenting conniver" and claimed that he had devoted his life to ruining him. In 1990, Rabin watched Peres corrupt the Knesset in what he called, "the stinking deal."

After the tie in the 1984 elections, Peres understood that his Labor Party could not win a national election because the 600,000 strong Moroccan community would never support its policies. But Peres saw a way around the problem. A new party, Shas, which represented Moroccan interests, had won a few seats in the Knesset. If the party could be corrupted and then financed to become a serious electoral force, Labor could win the Moroccan vote through the back door. He keyed in on 23 year old Arieh Deri, the secretary of the party's spiritual leader Rabbi Ovadiah Yosef. Peres sent his cronies Haim Ramon, Yossi Beilin and Moshe Shahal to flatter Deri, draw him into illegal business deals and further his career. Within a year, Deri was appointed Director of the Interior Ministry Office and by the age of 25, Peres arranged that he become the Minister of the Interior.

In 1990, Peres was the Minister of Finance in a unity government headed by Yitzhak Shamir. As Finance Minister, Peres recorded every agora of thefts Deri was perpetrating in the Interior Ministry and in February 1990, he decided that the moment had arrived to blackmail Shas.

Working with Secretary of State James Baker to bring down Shamir, he devised a plan to become Prime Minister. Baker presented a new peace plan, which included negotiations over Jerusalem. Peres and Baker both knew that Shamir would have to reject the plan. So Peres caused a government crisis by demanding that Israel, "Say yes to Baker." He ordered a non-confidence vote against his own government, knowing that he would win. He had sent his deputy Yossi Beilin to Deri with a full report of his thefts and gave him the choice of facing prison or felling Shamir. Deri chose the latter and led the once Rightist, Orthodox Shas Party to abstain from the vote. Shamir fell and Peres was given the right to form the new government, though this term only lasted 88 days. The blackmail of Shas, however, never desisted and the current peace process was built on the back of Peres' corruption of this hapless party.

* In February of 1994, Peres' friend, the French intellectual Marek Halter made an amazing admission to the Israeli newspaper *Chadashot*. He claimed that in May 1993, he delivered a letter from Peres to the Pope, promising that he would arrange Vatican political hegemony over the Old City of Jerusalem. The plan had the Vatican controlling the Holy City, with UN soldiers guarding the entrances.

As incredible as the story sounds, it was soon backed by solid proof. The Italian newspaper *Il Stampa* confirmed the Vatican deal and added that it was included as a secret clause of the Declaration of Principles signed with the PLO in September 1993.

In March 1995, the Israeli radio station Arutz Sheva, was given a copy of a cable between the Israeli Embassy in Rome and the Foreign Ministry in Jerusalem. This cable described the very promise to the Vatican in detail. The cable was reprinted on the front page of *Ha'aretz* within two days.

Trapped, Peres came up with a not so ingenious explanation. The cable was genuine, he explained, but someone had whited out the word "not." The cable really said that Israel would "not" hand over hegemony of the Old City to the Vatican. Incredibly, numerous Israeli rabbis who had previously cancelled their Passover invitations to Peres, accepted his goofball excuse and reinvited him to their tables. Another crisis passed with Peres emerging unscathed.

* In February 1994, the director of the Labor Party's publishing branch Bet Beryl, Mordechai Nessiyahu, was poised to release a powerful book on the peace process, exposing Peres' real role in Oslo. As publisher of Labor's own writers and employer of Peres' daughter at Bet Beryl, Nessiyahu was well positioned to know the secrets of Oslo. After the newspaper *Globes* reported that Nessiyahu's book would offer proof that Peres played no role in Oslo, Joel Bainerman, my co-editor of the newsletter *Inside Israel* and I decided to meet him.

Our meeting was in the cafe at the Habima Theater in Tel Aviv. Nessiyahu was a great supporter of Oslo and had no bones to pick with anyone but Peres. He explained that Rabin and Beilin had initiated Oslo behind Peres' back and both agreed that the talks in Norway had to be kept secret from Peres in order that he not sabotage them. The Oslo talks were sponsored by Washington/London and Peres was tied to France/Continental Europe, whose interests did not coincide with Rabin's. Rabin despised the French and during this period allowed Peres to concentrate on his French diplomacy knowing it would be fruitless.

According to Nessiyahu, Peres did not learn of the Oslo talks until April 1993, five months after the process had begun with a meeting in London in November 1992. After the talks were concluded with an agreement, Peres wrote a book including himself in the Oslo track. Nessiyahu told us, "He completely rewrote history. His book is a lie."

Not long after our interview, Nessiyahu's 30 year old son died in mysterious circumstances. His girlfriend explained, "We were sitting with friends and he just stopped breathing." If Nessiyahu's book was ever published, no one ever said anything about it.

*   Peres has turned Israel into a shelter for international black money. How he operates was illustrated in the case of the former Ukrainian President Yafim Zviagilski. In June 1994, Peres and Police Minister Moshe Shahal flew to the Ukraine and met with Zviagilski. Three months later, the Ukrainian leader arrived in Israel with over $30 million pilfered from his country's treasury.

He arrived on a visa given him by the Prime Minister's Liaison Office, called Nativ, the very same organization that had hired Yigal Amir, the fall guy for Rabin's murder, for work in Riga, Latvia for five months in 1992.

Naturally, the Ukrainian government protested and demanded the return of the money and extradition of the thief. Peres said he'd get right on the case and appointed Tzvi Hefetz, legal affairs advisor for Nativ, to investigate.

The Ukrainian president and his money are still hiding in Israel, as are similar crooks and their billions of stolen dollars from the former Yugoslavia, Poland and sundry nations elsewhere.

*   For years the rumor that Peres turned master spy Eli Cohen in to the Syrians has floated around Israel but few believed he was capable of betraying an Israeli agent. Then in 1994, newspapers in Jordan, Saudi Arabia and London published a report that makes the rumor believable. Adnan Yassin, as Yasir Arafat's security chief, was the highest-placed Mossad agent in the PLO. As a gesture of good faith to Arafat, the Arab newspapers reported that Peres blew Yassin's cover. Yassin's car was searched and high-tech communications equipment, as well as sophisticated explosives were found. He was shipped to Yemen and never heard of again.

*   It's just a matter of time before Peres' complicity in the Rabin assassination is revealed. There are already three books in the Israeli market which accuse Peres of being the mastermind behind the murder and the irrefutable proofs will be released during his term as President, if we allow him to be so appointed.

Natan Gefen in his book *Fatal Sting* reviews Peres' sick hatred for and jealousy of Rabin and offers a convincing argument that Peres was blackmailed by the Likud before the 1996 elections and forced to lose the race. I reached the same conclusion independently, after I was told the full story by two cabinet officials. As President, Peres will be subject to the same blackmail.

This is not the place to prove that Rabin was murdered by a few officers of the General Security Services (Shabak). For the uninitiated, just know that there are now five books out in Israel which make this claim and prove it. They are my book *Who Murdered Yitzhak Rabin*, *Fatal Sting* by Natan Gefen, *Srak* by Ori Barkan, *Lies: The Rabin Assassination and the Israeli Secret Service* by David Morrison and *Your Brother's Blood* by Michael Raz.

The Israeli public's growing awareness of the Shabak's complicity will explode during the term of the next presidency.

There may be a dozen people in Israel with the power and influence to order a political assassination on the level of Rabin's. Of them, only Peres appointed the primary suspects to high office. On the night of Rabin's assassination, Peres appointed the likely shooter, Yoram Rubin to command the Prime Minister's bodyguard unit. Late last year, Peres appointed the head of the Shabak at the time of the murder, Carmi Gillon, to the high-paying post of Chairman of the Peres Center for Peace. Note that on the night of the murder Gillon was in Paris, he admits, meeting with officials of French Intelligence.

Earlier this year the Zionist Organization of America released documentation that that the Abu Dis Agreement between Israel and the PLO, which divides Jerusalem was signed in Paris by Foreign Minister Peres twelve days before Rabin's assassination. Rabin was never informed of the signing.

Earlier, Peres' friend, the French media tycoon Jean Frydman agreed to finance the rally where Rabin died. There is a frightening document in the hands of responsible journalists that will be released in due time. It is an interview with Frydman in French in which he details how he and Peres sat with a most reluctant Rabin and finagled him into participating in the rally. Yet Rabin refused to attend until the last moment. Testimony from Rabin's regular driver Yeheskiel Sharabi has been uncovered and it will be released when the Rabin truth finally explodes.

Sharabi explains that 90 minutes before the rally, Rabin unexpectedly called him and told him not to pick him up. He would not be going to the rally. Sharabi offered to remain by his phone in case he changed his mind. But someone had already changed Rabin's plans. Instead of his regular chauffeur driving him, Rabin was driven by Peres' regular driver, Menachem Damti.

And it is the Damti connection that will be Peres' demise. Before anyone was supposed to be in Rabin's car, the back passenger door slammed. For the past four and a half years, researchers have known that someone was waiting for Rabin in his car, but only in the past year has that someone been likely identified. Damti invited several members of his family to be with him in the "sterile zone" and one of them, his twelve-year-old daughter, snuck into the back seat. She was an accidental witness to the murder and because she was there and had to be removed, Rabin's car was diverted for no less than twelve minutes before it finally arrived at the hospital.

We have Peres captured on videotape rounding Rabin's car, looking in the backseat and then stopping in front of the limousine. He stares intently into the backseat and calls his four bodyguards over, telling them to look into the backseat as well. All their heads turn towards it. They have no explanation for the passenger so Damti is called over to explain. Peres scolds him and Damti looks most perturbed, shaking his head back and forth vigorously. But it is too late to get her out. Peres looks towards the stairs and sees Rabin walking towards his car. There is no stopping the murder. Peres enters his own limousine and the murder carries on as planned, but with an unplanned witness in the backseat of Rabin's vehicle.

There is NO explaining Peres' actions except that he knew how the murder was supposed to be carried out. That is the only way he would have known that something was amiss in Rabin's Cadillac.

And that's not the only film of the night that traps Peres. At the emergency cabinet meeting Peres addressed the stunned nation with the words, "We sang the song and then Yitzhak put the songsheet in the side pocket of his jacket where the bullet pierced it."

The next day it was announced that Rabin was shot twice in the BACK. Only months later, when Rabin's medical records were retrieved by diligent researchers was it proven that Rabin was, in fact, shot from the front. On the night of the murder, only a very few close to Rabin's medical treatment knew about the frontal shot. So how did Peres know?

Our nation will not be able to withstand the trauma of a Peres presidency. We are in a fragile enough state without inviting the kind of social collapse that this atrocity will bring. The widespread perception that Peres murdered Rabin has led to a rumor heard throughout the nation. It goes like this: Peres is seeking the presidency to pardon himself when the Rabin truth emerges. It is his last refuge. Unfortunately, the Israeli people will not have the luxury of a similar refuge.

PERES TRAPPED BY HIS OWN WORDS

Last summer, a faithful correspondent from the American Northwest wrote to tell me, "I have a videotape of Shimon Peres agreeing with your claims. He must be very sorry he made this tape." The correspondent, Kevin, shipped me a videotape of a PBS documentary about the Middle East peace process. Within, Peres implicates himself deeply in the Rabin assassination.

After viewing the remarkable evidence, I decided to wait before showing it publicly. Wait for what, must be the readers' question. I answer, wait until I had gathered enough solid evidence proving Peres organized the murder of Yitzhak Rabin. Those who have been following my investigation over the past year know the devastating proof I have gathered. For those who haven't, here is the case summarized.

There are perhaps a dozen people in Israel with the power and influence to have organized the assassination of the Prime Minister. By 1997, I had proven who was involved in the operational side of the murder and they included Rabin's personal bodyguard Yoram Rubin, his driver on the fatal night Menachem Damti, and the head of the General Security Services (Shabak), Carmi Gillon. Of the most politically influential Israelis, Peres and only Peres had appointed these men to vital positions.

On the very eve of the murder, Peres appointed his driver Menachem Damti to replace Rabin's regular driver Yeheskiel Sharabi. I tracked down Sharabi's testimony to the Shamgar Commission of Inquiry in which he testified that Rabin called him ninety minutes before the rally and cancelled his services. Not knowing that Damti had replaced him, Sharabi told Rabin that he would remain on standby in case he changed his mind.

Not two hours after the murder, Peres appointed the "gallant" Yoram Rubin to command his own personal security unit. In late 1999, Peres appointed Gillon as chairman of his peace center and also appointed Meir Shamgar to sit on its board of governors.

In due time, I traced the authorization for the murder and its planning to the French government and its secret services. Half a year ago, the Zionist Organization of America released the terms of the Abu Dis agreement signed in Paris less than two weeks before Rabin's murder. Peres had agreed to divide Jerusalem and offered the PLO a state capital in the city. With this agreement in hand, and

116

withheld from Rabin, the French gave the final go-ahead for the assassination. Carmi Gillon spent the assassination night in Paris coordinating the post-murder program with French intelligence officers.

Two months ago, I was forwarded an article written by Jean Frydman for the *Paris Match* two weeks after the murder, in which he details how he and Peres persuaded a reluctant Rabin to attend their November 4th gathering and how he paid for and organized the security for the rally.

Peres had worked closely with the head of the Shabak, Rabin's driver, his bodyguard and the rally's financier, in other words, with all the main murder conspirators, and this could not possibly have been a coincidence. It was after receiving Frydman's unintended confession that I knew Peres was guilty. However, his guilt was by association and though the circumstantial evidence was overwhelming, what was missing was indisputable proof.

I decided then to release the film publicly and just as publicly, accuse Peres of murder. The right opportunity arrived in mid-August. I was invited to speak nine times in seven days to yeshiva students, their teachers and families who were on a brief vacation from their regimen of studies. The average crowd was over 200. Twice the audiences exceeded 350. I reached over 2000 people in a week and they saw the film clip in its entirety for the first time. When the clip ended, most of the audiences burst into impromptu, extended applause. Peres did indeed prove my case and everyone understood the significance of his words.

The PBS Film

Stock footage of overhead shot of the rally. Rabin and Peres sing *Song of Peace* on the podium.

Announcer: On the night Syria and Israel agreed to renew talks, a rally was held in Tel Aviv.

Peres: We sang, the three of us, the singer Miriam Aloni, Yitzhak and myself. Yitzhak and I are not great singers. He had the words of the peace song written on a sheet of paper. After we sang, Yitzhak folded it and put it in the pocket of his jacket.

Peres opens the left side of his jacket and puts the imaginary sheet inside the pocket.

Announcer: On the way to his car, he was shot dead by an Israeli extremist.

Peres: Three bullets went through his heart and through the songsheet.

Eitan Haber announces Rabin's death outside Ichilov Hospital. Yasir Arafat expresses his condolences.

Peres: We went to the room where he was lying on the bed. His body was covered in a sheet up to here.

Peres indicates to the chest.

Peres: On his face was an expression of peace and maybe irony. It was his typical Rabin smile.

Peres chokes up.

Peres: I kissed his forehead and said goodbye.

Announcer: Peres was now Prime Minister.

The Significance

The Shamgar Commission of Inquiry determined that Yigal Amir shot Rabin twice in the back. This is the official version of history as accepted by the government of Israel. I had collected Rabin's surgeon's report, his operation summary, his surgical review, as well as taped interviews with the Health Minister Ephraim Sneh and the Director General of Ichilov Hospital, Prof. Gabi Barabash from the night of the murder, which all indisputably stated that Rabin was not shot twice, but three times and not just in the back, but once frontally. This led to the inescapable conclusion that the Shamgar Commission issued a whitewash, because Amir did not shoot Rabin three times and never had an opportunity to shoot him from the front. Hence, someone else shot Rabin.

Now we know that Shimon Peres agrees with me because he is on tape saying that he was in Rabin's hospital room, viewed his body

118

and, with his own eyes, saw that he was shot three times, once from the front.

Thank you Shimon for verifying my work.

Now we must ask some hard questions. On the assassination night, Peres announced to the cabinet that Rabin was shot through the songsheet, a claim he repeated at the 30 day commemoration of the death. However, almost everyone felt he was being literary, creating an image of peace being murdered.

However, in January 1995, now-Prime Minister Shimon Peres testified at the Shamgar Commission and did not relate the story of the three wounds, nor of the frontal shot. Worse, far worse, Peres, as Prime Minister accepted the lying conclusions of the Shamgar Commission. If Israel's leader knew Rabin was not shot only twice in the back, why did he allow the commission's findings to be accepted as truthful by the Knesset? Why did he permit a lie to become history?

The Future Trial of Shimon Peres

The ideal trial of Peres, someday...

Prosecutor: Isn't it a fact that we have you on tape stating that you saw Rabin's corpse and that he was shot three times and frontally through the chest.

Peres: Yes but I didn't mean it.

Prosecutor: You mean you lied?

Peres: No, I was being dramatic. I didn't mean to be taken literally.

Prosecutor: Which part was not to be taken literally: the statement that Rabin put his songsheet in his jacket pocket?

Peres: No, I meant that.

Prosecutor: The statement that you viewed Rabin's body?

Peres: No, I saw it.

Prosecutor: The statement that he was shot three times? Was there some literary meaning in the number three that you wished to convey as a metaphor?

Peres: Perhaps. Three has many meanings. The holy trinity for example. Maybe I meant three figuratively, in a Christian sense. That's right. I saw Rabin as crucified. That's why I said three shots. Or maybe I meant three in the sense of the perfection of an equidistant triangle. That works too! And don't forget that three's a crowd. There are lots of reasons why I could have said three.

Prosecutor: So he really wasn't shot three times and a bullet didn't pass through the songsheet?

Peres: No, I was just kidding. Can't you take a joke?

In other words, Peres, in a fair trial, could never explain away this video clip in my possession. He is trapped by his own words. At a minimum, he knew how the murder really happened and for some reason, decided to allow a national lie to be propagated with Amir, the religious community and the residents of Judea and Samaria taking the rap for a murder they didn't commit.

Then there is the greater likelihood that he was covering his own complicity in the murder.

The Songsheet

Peres states that Rabin was shot through the songsheet. This is a lie and I'll prove it. Note the attached photograph of the songsheet and the superb analysis by Arthur Vered. His main points are:

* The sheet has been repeatedly folded. Rabin folded it once; why would he refold it over and over again?

* There is a round black stain, but no hole, in one corner of the sheet. Since the sheet was folded into quarters, a real bullet would have pierced the sheet four times.

* Had Rabin been shot through it, gravity would have pushed the blood down towards the bottom of the sheet. Instead, the darkest

stain is at the center and the spread is even. Hence, the blood was poured onto the sheet after it was removed from Rabin's pocket.

Vered concludes that the blood on the sheet is not Rabin's. Surprisingly, that is the suspicion of attorney Eyal Shomroni-Cohen, the lawyer for Shabak provocateur Avishai Raviv, currently on trial for not preventing Rabin's murder. He told me that he is pursuing similar lines as my own to prove his client's innocence and that he requested the songsheet from the court to test if Rabin's blood is actually soaked into it.

What does all this mean? My faithful readers know that the hospital records prove Rabin entered Ichilov with two back wounds, was revived and then shot a third time, this time frontally. My initial suspicion, which has been more than justified by later evidence, is that the plotters tried to produce evidence of a frontal shot by creating a hole through the sheet, in order to explain away Rabin's new wound. They started to make a fake bullet hole, realized the futility of faking evidence and took a new tack: threatening the doctors to change their public reports to two back wounds. This coverup began at approximately 2 AM when the state pathologist, Dr. Yehuda Hiss, wiped the third wound from his autopsy report.

The attempt to create a shot through the songsheet was known ONLY TO THE MURDER TEAM. Unless Peres can come up with a viable explanation of why he thought the bullet passed through the sheet, he must have been on the team.

Someday, in a better Israel, a prosecutor WILL ask Peres why he said Rabin was shot through the sheet. If he answers that he was given wrong information, the next question will be "BY WHOM?"

If not by the murderers, then who else? There is not one record of any doctor, nurse or police investigator who announced a shot through the songsheet. Only those who tampered with the sheet knew of the attempt to create a bullet hole in the paper and they had to have been in on the murder plot.

I wish Shimon Peres a long life, until 120, so he will have the opportunity to answer these questions in a courtroom and so will spend the rest of his days in prison, hopefully atoning for his crimes against Yitzhak Rabin and the Jewish people.

EPILOGUE

IT'S YOUR LAST CHANCE, STUPID JEWS!

Prime Minister Ehud Barak has just signed an agreement with arch-terrorist Yasir Arafat. The nightmare is back, Jews, but it never went away. You Jews will watch CNN and read the newspapers, it doesn't matter which, and you will be told a totally false history of how Barak chose to give up over 10% more of Judea and Samaria today. And in a few months, you will also get a totally false history from the same media about the next pullback...all the way to Jerusalem.

So here's what really happened and you Jews won't believe it because you've been made far too stupid to ever defend yourselves with the Truth.

You see, there is this small think tank in Manhattan called the Council on Foreign Relations. It only consists of 3000 members but Clinton is one of them, so are Gore and Dole. So has every President in the past generation been a member. And every Secretary of State and National Security Adviser. In fact, the CFR controls American foreign policy and is responsible for literally all the deliberate diplomatic fiascoes of the twentieth century.

Now, we know precisely what their plans are for Israel because they told us in their Middle East Task Force report of 1997. This task force was first chaired by William Cohen (CFR), but Clinton (CFR) asked him to become Secretary of Defense, so Henry Seigman (CFR) took over. And what are the findings of the CFR? Well, for starters, Israel has to withdraw to its 1948 borders and Jerusalem has to be divided to make room for a Palestinian capital.

In February 1995, Yitzhak Rabin chose Barak to be his successor, precisely because he was an incompetent IDF Chief of Staff, covered in scandal. He invited Barak to a private meeting with Warren Christopher (CFR) and the ball started rolling. By March, Barak was in America for four months of CFR training in preparation for his takeover of the Prime Minister's helm. He had some meetings with Henry Kissinger (CFR), Lawrence Tisch (CFR), and Edgar Bronfman (CFR) and they agreed to finance his ultimate election as Israeli Prime Minister. But, Blind Jews, there was a price and that price was complete adherence to the CFR's Middle East peace process.

123

In November 1995, Barak's rival, Shimon Peres, with operational guidance from the French secret service, murdered Yitzhak Rabin. This was a disaster for the CFR and they sent all their big guns to Rabin's funeral. Ford, Carter, Bush, and Clinton cornered Peres and warned him in no uncertain terms, and these people only employ certain terms, that Peres would make his party opponent Barak, Foreign Minister. That task done, the CFR determined that Peres would not win the next general election and they utilized every bloody trick in their murderous book to make sure of it.

They didn't mind. Netanyahu had long been purchased by them. It didn't matter who led Israel. The style would be different but the results the same. You see, CFR policy invariably leads to war, and I will not cite all the examples but recently their hands have been in Somalia, Rwanda, Angola, Kosovo, in fact all of former Yugoslavia, Panama...oh heck, it goes on and on. When they talk about a "peace" process, they mean a finely sculptured war process. And with the help of their many members in the major media, they create an unreal reality that seems hopeful and logical and one that Stupid Jews everywhere buy without a second thought.

Now, Netanyahu played ball early in his new administration but he got a little too guilt-ridden and stubborn by the middle. It was like pulling teeth getting him to cooperate in Israel's suicide. Still, by the end, he and the longtime leftist plant in the Likud Ariel Sharon did acquiesce at the Wye Plantation, owned by the Aspen Institute, a sister organization of the CFR. However, the CFR found the process too nerve-wracking with Netanyahu and they decided to send their finest team of brainwashers to Israel to get him out of power and Barak in. Their primary strategy was for Barak to keep his mouth shut during the campaign and let them turn Netanyahu into Satan.

The strategy was a winner for Barak but not for the so-called "pro-peace" camp. Barak's Labor Party won only 26 seats; it's ally to the left, Meretz won just 10 seats. That's all the Zionist left has sitting in the Knesset, 36 seats of 120. Even with his Arab "partners," who would be delighted to see Israel disbanded once and for all, Barak had no authority to shove Wye down the nation's throat.

Panicked by this result, George Schultz rushed to Israel and told Barak to co-opt as many political parties as possible to reduce the opposition to the miserable Likud. And he was further told to follow the instructions of the CFR's psychological team. He was to be seen acting tough and that would be arranged with the cooperation of

Arafat. A few minor crises would have to pass before the next stage of Israel's dismemberment took place. When the timing was right, Madeleine Albright (CFR) would make her move and the deal would be done.

Well, now that the ink is dry, Stupid Jews, you'd better smarten up in a hurry. The previous potted history is actually what happened, but the Stupid Jews will dismiss it as "conspiracy" theory. And that's par for the course this century. Barely fifty years ago, the Jews were forced to leave their European homes for ever decreasing space in distant regions, then they were squashed into ever more crowded ghettos, and finally into ever smaller camps. And the Stupid Jews cooperated, just as they are doing today.

But now Jews, you have about a week to get enlightened. And I have a way to get us out of this mess. You can forget fighting the government over the latest agreement. It's futile. And don't even try to expose the CFR's dastardly plots. You'll be a laughing stock because that's the way things have been manipulated against objective reality. You can't catch the diplomatic plotters in action.

Now if you want to reveal just how evil the "peace" with the PLO really is, expose the Rabin murder and NOW!!! On this one rare occasion, the plotters were caught and if there were a concerted effort, the murderers would not escape. We have all the documents from the hospital, police laboratory, courtroom and the crime scene and there is no other possible conclusion than that the convicted assassin could not physically have committed the crime. Hundreds of thousands of Smart Israelis now know the truth but have let the government and establishment media push them around for too long. If you want to save a viable remnant of the Jewish State, Jews you'd better push the issue and you haven't got much time. Like the original Oslo Accords, the latest disaster was signed just before the High Holidays when the Angry Jews are too busy to organize. That gives you about 72 hours to move.

I would suggest the following steps:

* Take my book *Who Murdered Yitzhak Rabin*, find the crime of your choice and issue a complaint at your local police station. Complain against the state pathologist altering the wounds reported by the doctors; (though we know they didn't), charge the police with doctoring evidence by finding that Rabin was shot point blank; charge Eitan Haber with withholding evidence from the police. There are

hundreds of crimes to be investigated; barrage the police with them using the documents in the book as the basis of the complaints.

* Spread the graffiti message, "Who Murdered Yitzhak Rabin" on every wall.

* Bombard the radio talk shows with opinions about Rabin's murder. Begin a mass letter writing campaign to newspapers, to the political parties, academia, etc., demanding that the public be told the facts.

* Print leaflets demanding that the public finally be told how Rabin died and place them on hotel counters, supermarket newspaper stands, restaurant message boards, in short, everywhere.

* Gather a few people and picket the Justice Ministry, demanding that the Rabin investigation be reopened.

* I have asked my publisher to send my book to every Knesset member. He has agreed. Do the same with anyone of influence that you know. Apply pressure from every quarter. Put them on the defensive over Rabin. And then go on the offensive over Wye.

Jews, you are my people and as stupid as I find so many of you, you're all I've got. The powers that be mean us no good, no good at all. The Smart Jews sense that but have no leadership and no direction. Smart Jews, you don't need leaders. You have the goods on Rabin's killers, that is your strength and the Bad Jews know it all too well. They also know that you can number their days in power if you corner them on Rabin. It is their Achilles Heel. And it is the only way of ending the century of the Stupid Jews.

BOOK REVIEWS

A ZIONIST LOOKS AT *FINAL JUDGEMENT*

Final Judgement by Michael Collins Piper has been ignored or viciously attacked by American Jewish organizations and media. No shock there since Piper makes a pretty cogent case for the Mossad being the moving force behind the assassination of JFK. I will attempt to redress this imbalance and offer a review of the book as a Zionist committed to the strength and survival of Israel.

To summarize early, Piper gets lots right and lots wrong. What is bothersome is it doesn't take much of what he gets right to make a case for Israeli involvement in the murder. Piper's central point, and it is a major revelation, is that Clay Shaw, Oswald's handler was on the board of a Geneva-based trade promotion company called Permindex, which I accept was a Mossad front for covert operations.

From this point Piper works backwards and connects Clay to the Mossad, the Mossad to Lansky and organized crime, Lansky to the CIA, the CIA to heroin production in South-East Asia, the heroin producers to the heroin processors of Marseilles, the processors to the OAS, the rebellious French intelligence outfit determined to assassinate De Gaulle for pulling out of Algeria, the OAS to the Mossad and now we've come full circle.

Kennedy infuriated Israeli Prime Minister David Ben Gurion by demanding an end to Israel's nuclear program. He equally infuriated organized crime by promising to end American involvement in Viet Nam, and thus cutting off its major source of raw opium. Even though he frightened many in the CIA with his declarations that the organization had to be replaced, and by his refusal to bring down Castro, that was not a prime motive in the assassination. The CIA was involved because its top gun James Angleton was an Israeli agent. His duty was to prepare the patsy and plant "false flags" in the Cuban exile community. In fact, even the alleged involvement of Italian Mafia leaders was a deliberate false flag as well. The real killers were OAS-employed Corsican hitmen, or at least one was for certain, and they were recruited by the Mossad's European chief assassin, Yitzhak Shamir.

I would dismiss the whole thing as a fantastic yarn, except four years ago I began researching the assassination of Yitzhak Rabin, and

I independently discovered too many facts in common with Piper's. The most uncanny is that I also conclude that French intelligence provided the operational guidance behind Rabin's murder.

I don't intend to retell *Final Judgement*. The following points are aimed at people who have already read Piper's book.

* I was already familiar with the Permindex story, having read Larouche literature. I'm not happy that he adopts the findings of a pro-Aryan organization whose primary purpose in life seems to be to destroy the British royal family. The fact that Piper is employed by the Liberty Lobby and their outlet, *Spotlight*, is not really thrilling to me either. Even less exciting are his quotes from Jewish traitors like Ostrovsky and Lilienthal. And now I will elaborate.

There is a superficial similarity between me and Victor Ostrovsky in that we both are exposing the misdeeds of Israeli intelligence agencies. The difference, and it is telling, is that he ran away to Canada to tell his tale, while I live and raise my family in Israel. His motives are highly suspect, mine are honest: I want my friends, family, and especially my children, to live in a better Israel for all ages.

That said, about half of Piper's sources are Jewish, and other than Gerald Posner, they are mostly respected assassination researchers. He is not at all reluctant to cite as an inspiration the Jewish investigator/attorney Mark Lane, and in fact Lane was not at all reluctant to represent *Spotlight* in a well-publicized legal action against the CIA. All in all, Piper doesn't sound like an anti-Semite and I can spot one. I believe he is a sincere truth seeker.

* The main difference between my research and his is I found the evidence to prove my case for Israeli secret service involvement in the Rabin murder. I gathered hundreds of pages of hospital, court and police records, combined them with indisputable first hand testimony and put together an airtight case. Piper does not succeed nearly as well. His argument, though deft IS all circumstantial. The weight of his circumstantial evidence is impressive but it is far from conclusive.

* Piper does not have a handle on the personal dynamics of Israeli politics. For example, he writes off Menachem Begin as a "terrorist." Wrong. He was a freedom fighter in the truest sense of the word and probably the only honorable person to serve as Israel's

Prime Minister. He somehow ties him into the plot because he had ties with gangster Mickey Cohen. Heck, everyone in Israel knows about these ties. Back in the late 40s when no one else would arm us, the gangsters used their muscle to save our fledgling state. So what?

But Piper intimates that just by knowing Cohen, Begin was in on the plot. That is out of the question. In 1948, Ben Gurion ordered Yitzhak Rabin to murder Begin on a ship called the Altalena. Begin would never have cooperated with Ben Gurion on a Hanukka party, let alone in the murder of an American president.

Ditto, Shamir. In the mid-1940s, Ben Gurion rounded up Shamir and his militia for the British and had them sent to incarceration camps in Central Africa. Admittedly, Shamir did work for the Mossad during Ben Gurion's regimes, but their personal ties were strained, to say the least. While Begin would never have cooperated with Ben Gurion in a presidential hit, it is almost as unlikely that Shamir would have. A better candidate would be Shimon Peres, Ben Gurion's close aide and the man who started the Israeli nuclear program with French collusion. He is suspect number one in the Rabin assassination.

* Piper mentions the well-known fact that Jack Ruby met with "Israeli journalists" at the Dallas police station the night before he finished off Oswald. Possibly enforcing Piper's claims, many of my correspondents have pointed out to me that in Leah Rabin's biography, she notes that her husband Yitzhak was in Dallas on November 22, 1963. And Rabin, himself, admitted that he was in Cambodia the next year inspecting an Israeli "experimental farm." Yes, Rabin could have been one of the "journalists" and yes, the farm could have been growing poppies.

That Rabin was up to his ears in drug running is illustrated during his tenure as Shimon Peres' Defense Minister from 1984-86. This was the era of Iran Contra and Israel was involved in selling arms to Iran to free American hostages. And the money was used to buy cocaine in Latin America, ship it to the US, use the profits to purchase arms and funnel these to the Contras.

Like Piper, Poindexter and North tried to shift the blame for the operation to Israel. Now being logical, Israel had its interests in the scheme; there was money and diplomatic brownie points. But Israel had no interest in freeing American prisoners or in funding the Contras. Iran Contra had to have been an American operation where the Israelis were called in for operational help.

I see the Kennedy assassination in the same terms. Oswald had been trained to be a stooge by American military intelligence from 1957, almost before the foundation of the Dimona Nuclear Reactor was even laid. Indeed, Ben Gurion could have been so angered by Kennedy's insistence on the dismemberment of Dimona that he agreed to contribute Mossad expertise to his assassination. However, the assassination's core plot was American and its genesis predated any possible Israeli involvement.

* By the same token, Piper implicates the Mossad in the murders of Americans who knew too much years after JFK was gone. William Colby's demise is his prime example. This implication dismisses the long list of political murders and murder attempts in the US since 1963, or for that matter, since at least Lincoln's time. There IS a culture of political murder in the US, it has been on high gear since Clinton has assumed power, it goes back at least 150 years and Israel, the Zionists and Mossad have nothing to do with it.

* Piper paints Israel as the murder and crime capital of the Middle East. May we remind him that assassination was the only means of changing Middle East regimes for a thousand years before Zionism emerged and that most of the hard drugs sold in Europe originate from the Syrian-controlled Beka Valley and Afghanistan. Israel didn't invent the rules of Middle Eastern politics and may well have been forced to adopt them to survive.

* Piper makes a connection between the JFK assassination and Israel's technical help in founding the Chinese nuclear program. While the fact of Sino/Israeli nuclear cooperation may be genuine, Piper fails totally to find its connection to Dealey Plaza. So why include it?

* Similarly, since 9 of 22 Warren Commission lawyers were Jews, they must have had an interest in the cover-up. Most specious is Piper's connection between Detroit multi-millionaire Max Fischer and Michigan Congressman Gerald Ford in the cover-up. As President, Ford was a disaster for Israel, twice withholding deliveries of fighter jets until Israel withdrew from positions in the Sinai and Golan Heights. He was no Israeli puppet and seemed to revel in pushing then-Prime Minister Yitzhak Rabin around.

If I would draw any conclusions, assuming Piper is right, it's that knowledge of Israel's involvement in the JFK assassination is being used to force Israel to commit suicide. How else can one explain Rabin's decision in 1993 to accede to American (i.e., CFR) demands and hand over the very heart of his nation to a ragtag band of terrorists and arm them to the teeth to boot? Perhaps Rabin's strange appearance in Dallas was the tool used against the Jewish people in the unstoppable American quest to make Israel defenseless.

* And one cannot ignore the strange demise of JFK Jr. Four witnesses saw the explosion that downed his plane. One was a reporter for the *Martha's Vineyard Times*. Kennedy radioed the airport tower that he was readying to land and then his plane fell 8000 feet in a few seconds. Yes, I'm sure he was murdered. And yes, the disastrous Israeli political establishment had one heck of a motive for involvement. The latest Kennedy to die violently was the only American editor to expose the true conspiracy behind Rabin's assassination. He did it in grand style in a 13 page article in the March 1997 issue of his magazine *George*. And he had every intention of continuing his exposes until he got to the bottom of the matter. We don't know what drove him to stand alone in seeking the Rabin truth, but it may have had much to do with the information contained within *Final Judgement*.

Let me conclude by observing that the Israeli public knew nothing whatsoever about how Rabin was really murdered until I took the trouble of explaining the truth to them. Today the polls show that 65% of my fellow Israelis want the Rabin assassination reinvestigated. We are waking up to the ugly reality of the kind of leadership we are saddled with.

But I take the opposite view of Piper: my research says America corrupted Israel and not the other way around. And, probably unlike Piper, I am seeking the truth so that one morning the rotten murderers Americans and Israelis call their political leaders will not make my country hopelessly unable to defend itself against even rottener forces.

WHY E.G. BAN BELIEVES
PEACE WILL NEVER COME TO THE MIDDLE EAST

A month ago I shared a book signing evening with E.G. Ban. He explained that the thesis of his book *The Constant Feud* is that political or any other kind of personalities have no ultimate effect on the Middle East. Without reading his work, I made the mistake of dismissing his idea as ridiculous. Now that I've read the book, I take it all back. He is on to something big.

Ban traces all the problems of today's Middle East to the end of the last Ice Age, 11,500 years ago. Until then the Middle East had been a rainy, fertile region, a near Garden of Eden. When the ice receded, the rains moved north and Europe became rich and fertile while the Middle East dried up. The sense of this loss and the resentment against the North for stealing the rain is imbued in the ancient myths of the region.

With the forests gone and most of the land turned to desert, the previous hunting civilization ended and agriculture replaced it. Animal husbandry allowed women to replace nursing with animal milk and the population exploded. The peoples of the region were forced to densely settle by the few large rivers and soon there was no river bank land remaining. The only option was to divert the river waters to interior lands and this required the first massive engineering projects. Only a strong tyrant could organize the irrigation works and allocate the water. Thus was born the hydraulic society, the precursor of Islamic fundamentalism.

Meanwhile in Europe, there was no need for backbreaking farming; water and game were plentiful. While the Middle East invented cities run by dictators, Europeans had the luxury of creating tribal democracies. If anyone objected to his life within his nation, there was little danger in leaving it. As the proverb goes: "The forest conceals, the desert reveals."

In Europe, the forest offered protection, while a man exposed in the desert has nowhere to hide. The only protection available was in the family or clan. And protection was vitally necessary, for the city-states that arose had little wealth beyond what could be accrued from their rivers. So beginning with Sargon I, these states organized massive raiding parties, the first international wars, to gain riches through looting. Hence was born the turmoil in today's Middle East.

Allow me to quote E.G. Ban.

On Islam:

"Islam is more than a religion. It is also a systematic and coherent ideology...It can be democratic, at least in theory, as all are equal before God, but it certainly cannot be liberal, as it cannot encompass universal human rights and freedom of conscience and religion...Islamic fundamentalism hits hardest apparently modernized societies, where traditional cultural values are most threatened. This is also why the countries of the Middle East cannot carry out a serious program of industrialization. Industrialization means capitalism, a systematic work order, and it would appear capitalism will not develop without a rational spirit...In contrast to the West, modern Islam has spread mainly among the cultural elite. It should be a sobering thought for Westerners to realize that most of those who received technical education in the West returned home strengthened in their Islamic beliefs, with all that it implies."

Honor in War:

"The people who lived in kleptocracies for so long, know well that to the victors, the spoils and they can do nothing about it. They also know that any mistake which the ruler might make will be carried to the bitter end, even when it was obvious a huge mistake was made. The occupation of Kuwait by Iraq, which caused the Gulf War, might be a good example. The honor-shame syndrome cannot allow anyone to admit errors and accept responsibility for them."

On the West:

"The hatred of the West is so universal and deep-seated that it does not need any encouragement from above. On the contrary, it is the people who keep a watchful eye upon their rulers not to fall into the error of coming to terms with the unbelievers."

On Their Leaders:

"The people know the rules of the game, realizing their best and probably only chance for a better life is to be on the winning side of the next change of regime. So when Westerners see on the TV screen a huge Eastern crowd cheering some obnoxious leader, it is not because they are made to do so. They love him, just as they loved Harun-ar-Rashid, Hammurabi and Sargon, as they loved the Pharaohs

133

and were proud of their achievements. They will love the next dictator too...The proverb "Better the Sultan we know" means that most of the people always love the present Sultan, lest he be replaced by someone worse...It is difficult to accept with any seriousness elections with victorious results of 99.996% of the vote. This does not mean to imply the elections were rigged...Genuine non-rigged elections could produce such results. It is the result of millennia-long brainwashing."

Summary of Middle Eastern Society

"* Law is what the ruler decrees.

* There are no independent centers of power, only the central authority.

* Place in society depends on family. Individual talent does not provide means of advancement up the social ladder.

* There is no ordinary way to change the social order.

* Rule is always a tyranny, mitigated by assassination."

THE OTHER RABIN MURDER BOOK:
A Review of Natan Gefen's *The Fatal Sting*

My expose of the true Rabin assassination, *Who Murdered Yitzhak Rabin*, received a great deal of attention because it was the first and because it was published in four languages. The release of a second book on the conspiracy, *The Fatal Sting* by Natan Gefen, was greeted with less fanfare, partly because that's what happens when you're number two, and in greater part, because so far, the book is only available in Hebrew.

Those who read Hebrew often ask if there is a rivalry between me and Gefen. The answer is no; we are on the same team. And I'm not being overly magnanimous when I conclude that his book is as valuable as mine for those seeking the truth of what really happened to Rabin. In fact, Gefen adds several documents missing from my work that round out the study of the assassination. Allow me to point out his most striking revelations.

Amir Did Not Confess at the Beginning

A month after the murder, on December 3, 1995, a court hearing was held to consider Israel Police's request for an extension of its investigation of the murder. Before the hearing began, Amir shouted at the reporters present, demanding to know why they were not investigating the murder of the security officer Yoav Kuriel. Most of Israel saw his outburst on television and heard the following interchange between him and Judge Dan Arbel, who ordered Amir to desist from speaking to the media.

From *Ma'ariv*, December 4, 1995:

One of the Reporters: Would you do it again?

Amir: Yes. After you understand why, you'll see the system is rotten. Everything is set up. What you're seeing is a facade. I didn't think they'd start killing people. Since Oslo B...

Judge Arbel: Don't talk about Oslo B. You're not the Foreign Minister.

Amir: They're killing people. Don't you understand that? It's all a lie.

135

Judge Arbel: What's a lie?

Amir: That I killed Rabin. I never even tried to kill him.

I included that remarkable exchange in my book but had no idea that Amir's denial appeared in the court records. Gefen managed to track down the protocols of this hearing and he reprints them in full in *The Fatal Sting*. After the reporters are removed from the court and the session continues on camera, Amir tells Judge Arbel:

> About the request for an extension, what you've seen now has all been a facade. I request to be allowed to explain the background to my actions. They're killing people. If you listen to the truth, the whole country will be up in arms.

Amazing it is that one month after the murder Amir was still trying to tell an Israeli court the truth and the judge turned down his request to speak. The justice system was rigged against Amir from the beginning and Gefen proves it. After this incident, Amir was taken away for over a month and a half and when he returned from Shabak prison to face the investigators of the Shamgar Commission and the judges at his own trial, he had changed. Now he was an ever-smiling buffoon who confessed every time a witness testified in his favor. If only Judge Arbel had let him speak the truth.

The Bullets

On page nine of his book, Gefen makes an astute observation about Hagai Amir and Dror Edni. Both were tried and given long prison sentences for supplying the ammunition to the murderer. Most of the case against them was based on the following events.

On the night of the murder, the police searched the Amir home in Herzliya and came up nearly empty-handed. Two days later, the Shabak (General Security Services, Israel's FBI), re-searched the home and came away with two pistols and a huge armory of bullets. Gefen observes that if Hagai Amir and Dror Edni were really involved in the assassination, they would never have left such an armory in the Amir house.

Now we jump to page 30 and Gefen reports on the bullet that supposedly shot Rabin's personal bodyguard, and my prime candidate as his murderer, Yoram Rubin. The actual bullet was never found and

Rubin was not actually shot. But traces of the bullet which passed through his jacket were found by Israel Crime Lab technician, Chief Lieutenant Baruch Gladstein, and he discovered brass, a metal that was not found in the bullets which wounded Rabin.

Gefen makes three points that I missed in my book.

* First, the prosecution explained away the different bullet by claiming that Amir loaded two types of bullets into his clip. Gefen puts the argument to rest by referring to the police ballistics report. No bullet with the chemical composition of that which pierced Rubin's suit was found in Amir's clip or in the armory allegedly kept by his brother Hagai and his "accomplice" Edni.

* Next, Gefen notes that hollowpoint bullets are rarely used in Israeli murders and it would have been mad for a political assassin to use them since they are much less effective at penetrating a bulletproof vest, which Rabin should have been but wasn't wearing. How would Amir have known Rabin wouldn't be wearing one? However, hollowpoints shatter upon impact and cannot be traced back to a specific weapon.

* Finally, a major revelation, nowhere in the court or police records are Amir's gun, clip or extant bullets tested for fingerprints. There is no fingerprint evidence that Amir ever held the murder weapon or loaded its clip. Gefen insists this could not have been an oversight and implies that the fingerprint evidence was deliberately withheld.

Tampering With the Film

Many people have found ways to prove that the "amateur" film of the murder, wrongly attributed to a Shabak flunkie named Ronnie Kempler, was obviously tampered with. The shooter in the still-frame from the film has a different haircut and face than Amir, is wearing a long-sleeved shirt, when Amir wore a short-sleeved shirt and is shooting with his left hand, while Amir shot from the right. It can't be Amir and I have concluded that someone else was superimposed into the frame to bring Amir closer to the point blank range the police found Rabin was shot at. Central to the case against Amir is the frame that supposedly captures the flash of the gun as he shoots. Bernard

Shechter, head of the Police Forensics Laboratory at the time of the assassination, told me that he had never seen a flash appear like that in any other shooting he had examined and suspected that it was drawn in. Arthur Vered, a computer expert pulled the flash frame from the Kempler film and placed it atop the flash still that was first published by *Yediot Ahronot*. They are not the same. Still, there are lingering suspicions that the gunflash was real.

Not any more. Gefen consulted a physicist who explained most rationally that the light generated by the flash of an ignited bullet cartridge is as brilliant as lightning. If the flash were real, it would have lit up Rabin's back, which it clearly does not. *The Fatal Sting* proves the photo of Amir shooting Rabin has been altered drastically.

Understanding Dr. Barabash

One of the biggest headaches I have when lecturing is explaining away the TV interview given by Ichilov Hospital director, Dr. Gabi Barabash on the evening of the assassination. While, the official version of Rabin's murder has him shot twice in the back, both Gefen and I agree that all the evidence proves that Rabin was shot three times, the final fatal shot coming from the front and ultimately shattering his spine, a wound the government claims never occurred.

I present two televised interviews from Ichilov to my audiences. First, I show Health Minister Ephraim Sneh announcing that Rabin was shot three times; in the chest, stomach and spinal cord. Then comes Barabash who confirms the chest to spine wound but claims Rabin was only shot twice.

The Fatal Sting more than suggests he was lying. Two hours later, Dr. Barabash was interviewed on Channel Two and he is much less certain about the number of shots. Gefen provides the text of this startling interview and keeps the original tape in his archive.

Channel Two Reporter: How many bullets are we talking about?

Dr. Barabash: Pardon me?

Channel Two Reporter: How many bullets are we talking about?

Dr. Barabash: I think two, no three, I think two. One of them injured the area around the heart and wounded the spinal cord, cutting it off.

Barabash can't get the story straight. He mixes up the cover-up with the truth.

When Was Rabin Shot?

The Fatal Sting includes a shocking document I had never seen before and frankly, I just can't digest it. I had concluded based on court testimony and hospital records that Rabin was shot at 9:40, placed in his limousine a few minutes later and arrived at the hospital at 9:52. Since the ride should have taken only a minute, I concluded that Rabin's driver, Menachem Damti, got unexplainably lost for eight minutes.

Two months ago, one of Rabin's surgeons, Dr. Kluger told *Ha'aretz* that, in fact, Rabin was twelve minutes late. How could I have been off by four minutes?

(I digress. A close associate of his informed me last week that Dr. Kluger has been afflicted by a mysterious malady and looks, "like a living corpse." He is the second doctor to be so mysteriously stricken recently. Last September, the head of Rabin's surgical team, Dr. Mordechai Gutman suffered neurological pain that left him unable to function for six weeks. The cause of the pain was never identified but my informant told me, "He got the hint.")

To confuse the issue more, Gefen presents the hospital conclusion based on blood coagulation that Rabin was shot 4-5 minutes before he arrived at Ichilov. This would mean, according to my published calculations, that Rabin was shot some three minutes after he entered his car. If Kluger is right, then Rabin was shot, some seven minutes into his final journey. This is just too much of a discrepancy and it must be explained.

Gefen does so in such a drastic fashion that, until I figure out what it means, I must remain speechless. Reprinted in *The Fatal Sting* are Amir's arrest records. According to them, he was arrested by the police at 9:30 PM, or a full ten minutes before, officially, Rabin was shot by him.

I tried and tried to work it out, until finally I phoned Nathan Gefen and asked him, "Is this arrest report mistaken? Didn't people check their watches to see when Rabin was shot? Why is it accepted that Rabin was shot at 9:40 if Amir was already in custody by then?"

He replied, "This is the first police report and it's the most authentic. After that, the arrest time was readjusted five minutes at a time to suit the cases of Shamgar and Amir's prosecutors."

In *The Fatal Sting*, Gefen quotes a police expert who explains that the time of arrest in such a form is the most vital information of all and it is rarely, if ever, so wrong. Gefen concludes, "If Amir had chosen to pursue his innocence, he has the best alibi of all. He was already under arrest when Rabin was shot."

There is much more in this book, but the arrest records shook me up the most. Gefen dares where I merely hinted: he names Shimon Peres as the organizer of the murder and he has strong arguments to back his accusation up. Today, I have even stronger ones than Gefen. However, the real strength of *The Fatal Sting* lies in the documentation, which when combined with the ample documents of my book, proves beyond any doubt that Yigal Amir could not possibly have murdered Rabin.

Last October, Rabin's son Yuval went on television and demanded a reinvestigation of his father's murder because, "If not, there are going to be a lot more books likes Chamish's soon." His prediction is, thankfully, coming true.

NOW THERE ARE FOUR

Just a year ago, my book *Who Murdered Yitzhak Rabin* was the only one to tell the truth about the assassination of Yitzhak Rabin. Now there are four.

Next came Natan Gefen's vitally important book *Fatal Sting*. In the past fortnight, two more books have entered the market, *Srak* by Ori Barkan and *Lies: The Rabin Assassination and the Israeli Secret Service* by David Morrison. I'll review both now, the latter at great length.

Last Friday Tsur Ehrlich wrote a fine review of *Srak* in *Makor Rishon*. I agreed with everything he wrote. He pointed out that this novelization of the Rabin murder conspiracy was written in 1997 and was based on the facts as known then. Since so much new information has emerged, the book suffers from a poor understanding of how the murder was organized. However, many unnoticed facts are sprinkled throughout the book and both Ehrlich and I were impressed that Barkan discovered that "amateur" filmmaker Ronnie Kempler and Rabin security adviser, later Mossad chief Danny Yatom, lived in the same apartment house. The obvious implication is that Kempler was invited into the plot by an insider.

Yet despite the obsolete data, Barkan creates a likely high-level conspiracy, of which Shimon Peres is at the top. I concur that he got that right, way before Natan Gefen and I came to the same conclusion based on far more groundbreaking research. Because he was so prescient, Ehrlich writes that Barkan must have intelligence ties and he concludes that, as a political thriller, "*Srak* is a pleasure to read."

Yesterday, I received an advance copy of *Lies* by David Morrison from his and my publisher, Gefen Books of Jerusalem. The book will be available to the public by the first week of June in both Hebrew and English. A massive poster campaign has been organized to publicize *Lies*. I predict this book will be the bombshell that cracks the Israeli government cover-up of the Rabin assassination.

Dr. David Morrison is a psychiatrist with a History degree. His style is to analyze crime like a patient on a couch. This works. The book's goal is to expose the lies the General Security Services (Shabak) have been spreading since Rabin's death and to make the reader understand why.

Morrison begins with the Bus 300 scandal and President Haim Herzog's 1986 immoral pardon of murderers and accomplices within the Shabak. Men of integrity were forced to leave the Service, while killers and liars kept their jobs, with the lesson that they are immune from prosecution, no matter how guilty, because their view of national security holds sway over the highest levels of the Israeli political system.

Next, Morrison reviews the rotten fruit of Herzog's pardon that led to the Rabin murder. He starts with Shabak head Carmi Gillon's sick hatred of the Right in Israel and how it led to unwarranted arrests and torture of totally innocent Jews. He focuses specifically on the violence of Avishai Raviv and the false arrests of seventeen active and reserve soldiers accused of transferring army weaponry to what turned out to be non-existent militias opposed to the Oslo Accord. In a gut-wrenching chapter, he interviews Lieutenant Oren Edri at length and he describes how the Shabak starved him, deprived him of sleep, threw him into a feces-smeared cell and when he finally collapsed into sleep, how his tormentors released nine hungry rats into the cell to gnaw at his face.

His tormentors were Carmi Gillon and Eli Barak, two chief conspirators in the Rabin assassination. Far more disturbing is the role another Barak had to have played in his torture and that of sixteen others in this phony underground. The IDF allowed its officer, Edri, to be taken away by the Shabak. The IDF had to have supplied false evidence of missing weapons to the Shabak to justify the arrest of so many soldiers. The IDF had to have known that the soldiers were innocent and yet, for political reasons of preserving the peace process by demonizing its detractors, readily availed itself to promote Carmi Gillon's ugly plot. And the head of the IDF at the time was Ehud Barak.

Ehud Barak was Chief-of-Staff during the heyday of Avishai Raviv's provocations, while the Kahalani brothers were deliberately bushwhacked into prison for a massacre of Arabs they never intended to perpetrate, while Shmuel Cytrin was incarcerated for months on end in solitary confinement for having the nerve to expose Raviv as a Shabak plant: and Ehud Barak was Chief-of-Staff at the time of the Hebron massacre, whose ties to the IDF are now being exposed by several Israeli investigators. The most recent research will draw numerous IDF officers into the Hebron swamp, including current Chief-of-Staff Shaul Mofaz, who has been reliably reported as meeting with Dr. Baruch Goldstein the day before he was set up as the patsy for the bloodshed.

Next, Morrison devotes many pages to an overview of the physical evidence which emerged after the Rabin assassination but was deliberately ignored by both the Shamgar Commission of Inquiry and the judges at Yigal Amir's trial. Not only does Morrison confirm the veracity of Natan Gefen and my findings, he adds essential new information as well. Most revealing is his interview with then-Israel Police Ballistics Lab head Bernard Shechter who explains convincingly why Amir could not have shot Rabin's bodyguard Yoram Rubin because the trajectory and the bullet were both all wrong.

I choose to focus on one aspect of *Lies* to give readers a taste of Morrison's style. He examines at great length "the conspiracy of silence" generated by the Shabak amongst Israel's leading media and political figures. By doing so, he finally explains why the Rabin family, which clearly understands that they are being lied to, and which had previously demanded a reinvestigation of the assassination, has chosen to join the conspiracy of silence. And Morrison explains why I have been the victim of such undeserving vilification by the Israeli establishment.

Morrison proves that the Israeli media is in the hands of the Shabak. He does so by referring back to the Bus 300 scandal. To hide its role in the murder of two shackled terrorists, the Shabak persuaded PM, at the time, Shimon Peres to call a meeting of the media Forum, a shadowy organization of media owners and ordered them to ban release of information about the scandal. All immediately complied. However, a new newspaper, *Chadashot,* was not a member of this cabal and released details of Bus 300. The government ordered the paper shut until its policy changed. The same tactics and the same personalities are shutting down Rabin murder evidence but are going much further this time around. They are also viciously attacking the advocates of "the conspiracy theory" and deliberately promulgating a fake alternative scenario, one that blames the religious community and its leaders for the murder. Morrison traces and proves this media sub-conspiracy convincingly. And it's about time someone did.

He begins by reviewing the only three Rabin conspiracy books available just two weeks ago: mine, Gefen's and Karpin and Friedman's book, paid for by Peace Now financier David Moshovitz, *In the Name of God; The Plot to Kill Yitzhak Rabin.* Of *Fatal Sting,* Morrison regrets that it hasn't been given the notice it deserves. But he has many nice words to say about me:

"When this author first heard about Chamish's thesis that Rabin was not killed by Amir, but was killed after he got into the car, he dismissed it out of hand as ridiculous. Who in his right mind would want to believe such a thing. After one examines the data Chamish cites, and verifies that it is, with minor exceptions, accurate, one still does not want to believe it but confronts 'difficulties in thought...'

"Karpin and Friedman cite Chamish's 'convoluted theories' about 'the angle of trajectory, the composition of explosives,' and those things sound very technical and not very interesting. One could posit that they want to discourage the reader from reading Chamish's book. They do not grapple with the abundance of data cited by Chamish that raises serious questions about the official version of Yitzhak Rabin's murder...

"So where is the 'plot to kill Yitzhak Rabin?' Karpin and Fiedman do not mention that Carmi Gillon's Shabak agents tortured army officer Oren Edri and a number of other religious settlers and still were unable to uncover any evidence of a religious, right-wing underground...

"If we have the whole truth, we may also have proof that Karpin and Friedman and other left-wing, secular elements participated in the cover-up, possibly in an obstruction of justice."

And Morrison is just as good at exposing the lies of a variety of Israeli journalists like Dan Margalit, Yoel Marcus, Hirsh Goodman, etc. *The Jerusalem Report* comes in for special treatment because it actually published a whole cover-up book. *Lies* exposes some of the more blatant falsehoods *The Jerusalem Report*'s staff must have known about but included anyway and concludes that only the book's amateurish writing saved it from being accepted as a legitimate account of the Rabin murder.

Morrison's own feeling about the Shabak-orchestrated campaign of lies in the Israeli media is:

"The Israeli media will stand exposed as a willing agent of the power structure, or participant in the power structure that has something to hide." When it does, "Each element of society, each in its own way, will have an opportunity to purge themselves of the corrupt elements in their leadership and choose new leaders to represent them...

144

"One could argue that full disclosure of the truth would only increase the schisms in Israeli society. Another view is that it could have exactly the opposite effect. Instead of exacerbating the splits in Israeli society, it may bring together the many components of the culture. It may unite them together against the common enemy - the elite of all the groups, those with the most to lose if the full truth emerges."

The time has come for all Israelis of honor to say, "Amen," to Morrison's wisdom.

YOUR BROTHER'S BLOOD
The Fifth Honest Rabin Assassination Book

Just a year ago, there was only one truthful book about the Rabin assassination, mine called *Who Murdered Yitzhak Rabin*. Now there are five, listed at the end of this review. Michael Raz Steinkrycer, better known as just Michael Raz, is a former police investigator, whose book *Your Brother's Blood* traces the Rabin assassination back to 1924, when a religious leader named Dahan was murdered by the socialist Haganah for arranging a peace track with Arab religious leaders. Since then, anyone who challenged the authority of the Bolshevist founders became a candidate for murder by the enforcement arm of the Labor Zionists, the Shabak.

Raz's book has precisely the same theme as David Morrison's *Lies: The Rabin Assassination and the Israeli Secret Service* and covers some of the same ground, i.e., Bus 300, the false arrests of 17 soldiers in 1994 for allegedly stealing army weapons to be used by a non-existent right wing underground. However, *Your Brother's Blood* enters realms where Morrison feared to tread such as:

* the wrongful imprisonment of Amos Baranes to cover up a Shabak officer's murder of the soldier Rachel Heller

* the corrupt dominance of Yossi Ginosar and his perjury which led to the long incarceration of a Druze army officer Izat Nafso

* the ugly suppression of Rabbi Uzi Meshulum and his congregation who dared to expose the kidnappings of thousands of— mostly Yemenite—infants in the early days of the state.

This approach is invaluable to understanding how the mechanism of the Rabin murder cover-up works. Take the Baranes case. Though it was obvious that Rachel Heller's boyfriend, a Shabak agent named Bichovsky was the murderer, a stooge was set up to take the fall. None of this could have happened without the approval and authorization of State Attorney General Meir Shamgar, who was later called on by the Shabak to cover up the truth of the Hebron massacre and turn Baruch Goldstein into the fall guy, and then the Rabin assassination, this time making Yigal Amir the victim for another Shabak murder.

146

Like Morrison, Raz relies heavily on documentation supplied to him by me and Natan Gefen but comes up with some powerful new evidence as well. Here are a few examples of how each Rabin book injects vital new information into the investigation.

First, Raz finally sheds light on the mystery man of the murder operation, Yekhezkiel "Chezi" Kalo. While it is universally known that Shabak provocateurs Avishai Raviv and Yigal Amir were employed by the Jewish Department based in Hebron, the chain of command is still fuzzy. Their immediate superior was Eli Barak, head of this department and we know lots about him. He is a wife swapper, stalker, drunk driver, wife beater and liar. In his most publicized act of debauchery, he stalked the reporter Carmela Menashe. One of his group of wife swappers in the suburban town of Kochav Yair was murdered in New York at the same time Barak was visiting there. After smashing his car while drunk, Barak lied to the police and testified that his passenger was behind the wheel. All in all, we have a picture of a violent misfit, just the type of personality who would murder for peace.

But, of Kalo, we knew next to nothing until the publication of the Raz book. We knew he was head of the Non-Arab Anti-Subversive Department of the Shabak and that he was Eli Barak's superior officer. How this department differs from Barak's is still covered in mystery. A year and a half ago, a terrified Kalo went public and in radio interviews and an infamous newspaper article, claimed he didn't know Avishai Raviv and was separated from him by eight officers in the Shabak's chain of command. Being kind, the approach didn't wash. No matter how many underlings dealt with Raviv on a continuing basis, he was their commander.

Now look what Raz reveals about him. He is not merely religious, but a graduate of a Bnei Akiva yeshiva, the very organization which supplies Judea and Samaria with many, if not most, of its Jewish residents. In fact, the principal of Kalo's yeshiva was the fiery Knesset member, Rabbi Ba-Gad.

So far, Kalo is merely a betrayer of his community. But let the following fact sink in deep. While Yigal Amir was in Riga, Latvia receiving Shabak training in 1992, Kalo was the Shabak officer in charge of security for the region!!! It sure looks like he was in on the Amir recruitment and subsequent exploitation from the very first day.

Then there is the dilemma of Health Minister Dr. Ephraim Sneh. In one of the most damning incidents of the murder, Sneh, then Health

Minister, announced Rabin's murder on television truthfully, saying, "He was shot three times; in the chest, stomach and spinal cord."

However, that moment of truth passed quickly and Sneh turned into a vocal and active leader of the murder cover-up. On October 6, 1996, Channel Two devoted a long and nasty report on my research and it was Sneh who called the TV station immediately, labeled me a "fantasizer" and personally intervened to have my lectures banned at the government-sponsored Israel Center in Jerusalem.

A year later, Sneh was interviewed in the now-famous NBC-*Extra* report on the conspiracy, and he gave his equally famous answer, "If I said two bullets or three one hour after the assassination, I think, is not important." The minions who have seen that response all react the same way: "Did he really say it wasn't important if Rabin was shot with two or three bullets????"

Michael Raz has uncovered a television interview with Sneh, which unveils his true feelings on the subject of Rabin's demise. He asked the question obvious to everyone investigating the murder; "The fact that Rabin received 21 units of blood testifies to the seriousness of his wounds. Keeping that in mind, why wasn't there even a drop of his blood found at the murder scene?"

Raz eliminates Sneh as an active conspirator but makes his ultimate role in the cover-up even more cynical and heartless.

And Raz concludes with the approach of a police investigator. He notes that all the digging and speculation are unnecessary.

> "The truth of the murder can be solved in one afternoon if polygraph tests were administered to (Shabak head) Carmi Gillon, (State Pathologist) Dr. Yehuda Hiss, (Rabin bodyguard) Yoram Rubin and (murder filmmaker) Ronnie Kempler."

I would add Shimon Peres to the list but that will be for the next edition of *Your Brother's Blood*.

Last week, the Israeli book chain monopoly Steimatzky refused to stock the upcoming new English language edition of my book *Who Murdered Yitzhak Rabin*. After numerous complaints, here is the stock letter they have been sending to the complainants:

Re: *Who Murdered Yitzhak Rabin* by Barry Chamish

With the flood of information and the flood of books being published, every author craves attention and tries to create artificial scandals in order to get that attention.

The book of Barry Chamish is being sold in our book shops in Hebrew and when it was originally published, it was also sold in English and re-ordered several times.

The demand today does not justify re-ordering. Commercial and professional considerations guide us when to stop re-ordering a book, as we eventually stop re-ordering books published in past years to make room for new titles.

Millions of book titles published around the globe are not available in our shops and millions of authors are being denied. We pick the titles which in our opinion will be most appealing to our customers and deserve the expensive import handling. Similar selection is made by every retailer, whatever his field, including all booksellers.

What the author is asking for is preferential treatment and undue promotion of his book that would give him financial benefit. This he hopes to achieve, not by paying for extra exposure, but by "bullying" letters, and false claims of censorship.

Still, if you wish to obtain the book, we can get it for you. Please send us a payment order by credit card of $35.- with your complete mailing address and we will arrange delivery.

Sincerely yours

Steimatzky Ltd.

Go into any Steimatzky store and you will find it is well stocked with twenty and thirty year old books by the likes of Golda Meir, Haim Herzog, AB Yehoshua, Amos Oz and the likes. However, the same chain cannot store even ONE book of mine, just in case someone should ask for it.

Here is the list of truthful Rabin books now on the Israeli market:

Who Murdered Yitzhak Rabin by Barry Chamish
Fatal Sting by Natan Gefen
Srak by Ori Barkan
Lies: The Rabin Assassination and the Israeli Secret Service by
    David Morrison
Your Bother's Blood by Michael Raz Steinkrycer

Please, go into your local branch of Steimatzky and try to find even one of these books. You'll see it is not merely me they are discriminating against; they are active agents of the Rabin cover-up. Boycott them until they serve the Israeli public as we deserve.

INDEX

151